THE
INNER GAME
OF
INVESTING

Books in the Wiley Investment Series

Cyber-Investing: Cracking Wall Street with Your PC, Second Edition
David L. Brown and Kassandra Bentley

The Investor's Anthology: Original Ideas from the Industry's Greatest Minds
Charles D. Ellis with James R. Vertin

Mutual Funds on the Net: Making Money Online
Paul B. Farrell

It Was a Very Good Year: Extraordinary Moments in Stock Market History
Martin S. Fridson

Independently Wealthy: How to Build Wealth in the New Economic Era
Robert Goodman

The Conservative Investor's Guide to Trading Options
LeRoy Gross

The Psychology of Investing
Lawrence E. Lifson and Richard A. Geist

Merton Miller on Derivatives
Merton Miller

REITs: Building Your Profits with Real Estate Investment Trusts
John Mullaney

The Inner Game of Investing: Access the Power of Your Investment Personality
Derrick Niederman

Patterns in the Dark: Understanding Risk and Financial Crisis with Complexity Theory
Edgar E. Peters

The Art of Short Selling
Kathryn F. Staley

The Stock Market, Seventh Edition
Richard J. Teweles and Edward S. Bradley

Market Magic: Riding the Greatest Bull Market of the Century
Louise Yamada

THE
INNER GAME
OF
INVESTING

Access the Power of
Your Investment Personality

DERRICK NIEDERMAN

John Wiley & Sons, Inc.

New York • Chichester • Weinheim • Brisbane • Singapore • Toronto

Copyright © 1999 by Derrick Niederman. All rights reserved.

Published by John Wiley & Sons, Inc.
Published simultaneously in Canada.

This publication is designed to provide accurate and authoritative information in regard to the subject matter covered. It is sold with the understanding that the publisher is not engaged in rendering professional services. If professional advice or other expert assistance is required, the services of a competent professional person should be sought.

Library of Congress Cataloging-in-Publication Data:

Niederman, Derrick.
   The inner game of investing : access the power of your investment
personality / Derrick Niederman.
      p.   cm. — (Wiley investment series)
   Includes index.
   ISBN 0-471-31479-X (cloth : alk. paper)
   1. Investments—Psychological aspects. I. Title. II. Series.
HG4515.15.N54   1999
332.6—dc21   98-51036

Printed in the United States of America.

10 9 8 7 6 5 4 3 2 1

To Peggy,
who got me started.

ACKNOWLEDGMENTS

This book was a pleasure to write, but along the way I accumulated more than a few debts. Let me begin by thanking everyone at John Wiley & Sons who helped bring this project together. Myles Thompson was the first to see my proposal, and he had the good sense to bring it Mina Samuels, who became my editor. Mina, your enthusiasm was contagious and your direction was superb. Thanks. On the production side, I'd like to thank Mary Daniello, as well as Nancy Marcus Land and Charlotte Saikia at Publications Development Company of Texas. They're the ones who converted a raw manuscript into a splendid-looking book.

Michael Gmitter of Securities Research Corporation supplied the charts for the book. For the cartoons, I am indebted to Jill Frisch of *The New Yorker,* Merrideth Miller of the Cartoon Bank, and Leigh Montville at Condé Nast.

My agent, Charles Everitt, represented the *Inner Game* proposal with distinction, and he certainly got it to the right place. I couldn't ask for anything more.

My conversations in putting the book together were numerous. I'd like to thank Glenn Greenberg, Dick Wood, Dave Cameron, Bob Malloy, Jay Nelson, Alison Mui, Louise Yamada, Howard Schilit, Mike

Mendelsohn, Roger Weiss, Arthur Kravitz, Alex McNeil, and Steve Syre
for their time and help, which ranged from providing terrific stories
to tracking down some ridiculous pieces of minutiae. Everything
counted.

Finally, I'd like to thank Timothy Gallwey, whose *Inner Game of
Tennis* debuted a quarter-century ago. If my title is a trifle less than
original, may my book at least match up well alongside the one that
started it all.

D. N.

CONTENTS

INTRODUCTION

It is a fact of investment life that most people aren't satisfied with their stock market performance. And wanting to do better is the American way. So what do we do? Do we work harder? Do more research?

If the answer were that simple, there would be millionaires on every street corner, because there is no shortage of investors willing to work hard to achieve superior results. But mere analytical prowess is not enough unless we understand the personal and psychological attributes that can either contribute to our investment success or make that success hard to come by. The plain truth is that anyone who is willing to examine his or her own personal foibles can become a much better investor. That's what this book is all about.

Consider Warren Buffett and George Soros, two of the greatest investors of the twentieth century. Though linked by their stock market successes, the two men have *absolutely nothing in common* other than their dedication to their chosen styles. Buffett is the consummate buy-and-hold strategist, whose holdings are almost exclusively well-known, large-capitalization companies such as Coca-Cola, American Express, and Gillette. Soros, on the other hand, is the mercurial trader, willing to make huge short-term bets on currencies, futures, emerging markets, you name it. The point is that each of these legends invests in a way that comes naturally. If Buffett tried to emulate Soros, he'd be a dismal failure, and vice versa.

That point sounds obvious, doesn't it? Yet so much of our investment literature doles out advice along the lines of "Do this," "Don't do that," or simply "Be like me," the idea being that the advice has worked wonderfully for the person who is doing the writing. All well and good, but many readers aren't psychologically positioned to convert those good words into action. For example, to tell someone "Don't buy a stock on a hot tip"—advice with which no expert would disagree—just isn't enough, because it ignores the question of why people feel inclined to act on those tips in the first place. Does Alcoholics Anonymous reach out to its members by merely saying "Stop drinking," as if those words alone will do the trick? Of course not, and the same principles apply to the investment world: You can't break your bad habits without knowing a little more about them.

Over the past 15 years, I have had the privilege of watching a wide variety of investors—from private citizens to magazine editorial boards, from neighborhood investment clubs to institutional investment committees. And at every step along the way I have found that personalities make their mark on investment styles.

I think of Glenn Greenberg, a friend, an erstwhile rival on the tournament squash circuit, and a codirector (with John Shapiro) of Chieftain Capital, an investment firm that made its name by seeking out a select group of companies with highly predictable cash flows: shipping company Gotaas-Larsen, oil service company Tidewater, timber company Burlington Resources to name a few. Chieftain buys, waits for Wall Street to catch on, then waits some more. But the style isn't for everybody. Just months after the firm's founding in 1984, two members of a flagship investing family bailed out. Interest rates were rising, their portfolios were down almost 20 percent, and the "sit tight and wait" philosophy sounded somewhere between stale and downright bogus.

But a third family member held on after a little thought, and 15 years later he remained a client—small wonder, for his holdings were worth 23 times what he started with. Beyond the virtue of patience, the unstated message is that you can be wrong about hundreds of stocks (namely, the growth stocks Chieftain sneered at throughout some glorious runs in the 1990s) and still succeed, as long as you have the wherewithal to make the most of your chosen strategy.

Then there's Gretchen Morgenson, a veteran financial writer *(Forbes,* the *New York Times)* and a former colleague of mine at *Worth* magazine. Gretchen vaulted to stardom with some outstanding exposes: On the macro level, she delivered a watershed proclamation of "Brand Names are Dead" back in 1991, well ahead of the so-called "generic craze" that forced consumer companies such as Kellogg, Procter & Gamble, and Bausch & Lomb to slash the prices of their products—and see their earnings and share prices stagnate. On the micro level, Gretchen dissected the flagging fortunes of Canadian bottler Cott Corporation in 1994 and opined that the worst was yet to come. Was it ever! Finding potholes in a bull market is a perilous practice, though, and Morgenson's supremely negative piece on computer stocks in late 1994 was too much of a good thing. Compaq and Dell defied her doomsday scenario and rallied by an average of 600 percent in the next three years. No one is right all the time, of course, but when caution is in your blood, selling too soon is a constant pitfall.

Sell-too-sooners might consider morphing their investment traits with my father, a savvy part-time investor who has a history of beating the Street to some undiscovered gems: Damon Corporation in 1982, before the first biotech boom; Carter-Wallace in 1990, sensing that AIDS and condoms were going to increase the company's profile; and, best of all, the Haloid Company—soon to become Xerox—circa 1960. Unfortunately, these brilliant insights were sometimes offset by his reluctance to get out when the times were good—as when biotech companies soared to 100 times earnings and condoms became a mania of their own. His problem was that selling during these peaks would have stripped him of his cherished label of "long-term investor." That's right—his gains came too quickly.

Of course, it would be a mite churlish of me to scrutinize colleagues and family while introducing a new book without confessing that my single biggest source of idiosyncratic investment behavior is, well, me. When I started in the investment business in 1982 as the proverbial lowly analyst, I found it easy to glom on to underdog stocks like Chrysler or less-celebrated winners such as shoe manufacturer Cherokee Group—a 20 percent grower whose stock sat at just four times earnings before Wall Street atoned for its neglect. Not bad for a beginner, right?

Meanwhile, though, I harbored pathological aversions to fabulous companies such as McDonald's and Coca-Cola (which, after all, *anyone* could buy). I thought I was being contrarian, when in fact I was just closed-minded. By the time the 1980s rolled to a close, I couldn't help but feel that my isolated successes had been dwarfed by the ones I let slip away, to say nothing of a few offbeat selections that remained offbeat years later. Looking back, I desperately needed someone to help me get out of my own way.

As unpleasant as these realizations were, by then I was fortunate enough to have landed a role as a stock market columnist at Fidelity, from which perch I could make amends. For starters, I ended up successfully recommending many of the stocks I had once avoided. (Can you imagine the results if I hadn't stuck up my nose the first, second, and third times around?) Then, recognizing that my own shortcomings ran the gamut from misplaced contrarianism all the way to outright gullibility, I began to dream about what it would take to create the perfect investor. If you could only reassemble the strengths of the various investment types we've just looked at, you'd be unstoppable.

But guess what? You can't do it. It's impossible to be everything to everybody. What *is* possible is to better understand how various personality quirks and predispositions interact with that maelstrom of activity known as the stock market. After all, there are only a finite number of mistakes that we can make: We can sell too soon, we can buy too late, we can hold on too long, and perhaps we can commit few other sins along the way. But for any one investor, some mistakes are far more likely than others. Recognizing and eliminating those mistakes is the major theme of this book. With any luck, you'll be able to identify your stock market personality a whole lot quicker than I did. I'm envious already.

SOME MARKET BASICS

Although the title of this section is "some market basics," you might be surprised to hear that I have no intention of talking about dividend yields, market multiples, debt/equity ratios, or any of the other various terms of Wall Street. Those can all wait.

In order to place our discussion of psychology and the stock market on the proper wavelength, there are really only two comments that I need to make up front. The first comment is that the market is not crazy. The second is that the market is not efficient. As long as these comments can be backed up, we'll be free to set some strategies in motion. Here goes:

The Market Is Not Crazy

If you've followed the stock market to any degree, you've surely encountered situations in which a company reports terrific quarterly earnings, only to see its stock *fall* five points on the news. Events like these give the market a bad name. Even worse, they give new investors the impression that the link between corporate performance and stock-price behavior is tenuous or even inverted. But that's not so. My proposition for the day is that good is good and bad is bad, even where the stock market is concerned.

So how can a stock plummet in the wake of a favorable earnings report? Probably because one of the following has taken place:

- The announcement of the most recent quarterly earnings (the good news) was balanced by a cautious outlook from the chairman for the quarter ahead (the bad news). Lo and behold, the market was reacting to the forward-looking bad-news component of the press release, not the backward-looking good part.

- The earnings, though perhaps good relative to other companies or to the market as a whole, came in below the expectations for the company in question.

- The stock had already gone up a lot in anticipation of the event, and some investors decided to take profits once the news was out.

Okay, what about the reverse situation? A company announces that it will lay off 5,000 workers, and its stock soars. How perverse is that? Well, when the market reacts positively to layoffs, the underlying logic is simply that a smaller workforce will translate into lower costs and therefore higher earnings. Note that this good-is-good reaction is typically reserved for stodgy companies in low-growth businesses, where bottom-line improvements are more likely to come from newfound efficiencies than from an upward spike in sales. When a young *growth* company reverses field and announces cutbacks (invariably because its hoped-for growth did not materialize), Wall Street isn't nearly as happy.

Is there really anything so strange about these reactions? Not at all. Yet the weird combination of zig and zag often sticks in our minds purely because of the timing of the reportage: when a company reports its earnings or announces layoffs, that's *news;* and when we see the stock acting a little funny *at that time,* an impression is made. Unfortunately, we almost always lack the background information that might have put the stock's behavior in perspective. My first encounter with the zigzag phenomenon was in 1983 when I happened to notice Liz Claiborne shares down five points (almost 20 percent) following an earnings release that looked pretty good to this newcomer. Little did I know that the stock's falloff was a mere blip in what became a 10-fold gain over five years.

You see, none of the foregoing suggested that the market's short-term reactions were *correct*. The market is capable of being dreadfully wrong for months at a time, even years. But there's a big difference between a mistaken reaction—which can be the source of future opportunity—and the image of a bad-is-good reaction, which makes some investors throw up their hands and denounce the stock market game as one of luck. It's not so.

The Market Is Not Efficient

The other hurdle we have to overcome lies at the opposite extreme, wherein investors view the market not as a den of perversity but as an all-knowing soothsayer. Some people fall into this trap because of a fatuous ivory tower invention called the *efficient market theory* (or EMT), which maintains that all publicly available information concerning a company is already woven into the price of its stock. This theory is not only false, it's dangerous. It implies either that you can't consistently beat the market without inside information or that research is expendable because everyone else is doing it. Nonsense. As a former academic, I take particular delight in saying that the efficient market theory* is an absolute pile of hooey, a claim that will be backed up at countless points within this book.

Yes, the market *tries* to be efficient. It *tries* to react to events as they occur. Yet the market's progress toward efficiency is inevitably futile for the simple reason that investors are human beings.

---

* It's sometimes called the *efficient market hypothesis,* but there's no need to get into the fine points of when a hypothesis becomes a theory.

If you are selling your house, you are unequivocally better off if your windows are squeaky clean, your rugs vacuumed, your plaster holes touched up, and so on. Attending to these simple and inexpensive items is recommended by any real estate agent still in business. In theory, a savvy house buyer could see through the facade and appraise these improvements at face value, but it doesn't work that way. Evidence is worth much more than mere possibility.

Try as we might, there is a limit to our ability to discount the future. When actors and actresses land important roles, they are understandably excited; they, like the market, react favorably to good news. But did Henry Winkler fully appreciate what lay in store the day he was tapped to play Fonzie in *Happy Days*? And what about Goldie Hawn in *Laugh-In* or Jason Alexander in *Seinfeld*? Think of how many times you've seen a stock go up four points on some pivotal news and marveled at the market's efficiency. But if you happened to look at those same companies a few years later, you might find that the favorable news was really worth 30 points or even more.

The downside is no different. Legend has it that the designer of the *Titanic* knew immediately upon hearing the extent of the damage that his beloved ship was doomed. But do you suppose that his initial reactions truly embraced all of his future emotions—such as when the ship lurched toward 90 degrees and began its descent to the bottom of the Atlantic? Did he appreciate right then and there that the disaster would rivet the globe for an entire century? Not a chance.

For a stock market equivalent of going down with the ship, let's go back to 1993, to a company called Lomas Financial. Lomas was in the mortgage-servicing business, and its primary asset was its mortgage portfolio. The only problem was that a sharp decline in interest rates was causing this portfolio to wither away as homeowners refinanced their mortgages. Even worse, the exodus of mortgages brought an immediate end to the company's apparent profitability, which had been created by stretching their costs over the lives of the held mortgages, a period that was shrinking before their eyes. Toss in some reckless spending and some high-risk swap deals gone sour, and you had a complete disaster. Small wonder that every Wall Street analyst who followed the company gave it the lowest rating possible. The stock traded for all of $7 per share when I first came across it, well off its earlier highs.

For those who believed in the efficient market theory, there was no reason to act; surely the market understood the company's dicey financial position. Not being a believer, I had no trouble putting Lomas on the monthly "Ten Stocks to Avoid" list I was running for *Worth* magazine. Two years later, Lomas shares were trading at $3/4$, as in *seventy-five cents per share*. For those keeping score at home, that's a decline of almost 90 percent, even after the public availability of all the negative information that inexorably sank the Lomas ship.

The reason such declines are possible is that investors can be shockingly slow to throw in the towel. Many Lomas diehards were doubtless unfamiliar with the fine points of cost amortization—not a grievous fault in modern society, but not quite as forgivable among shareholders of a mortgage-servicing company. In addition, a meaningful percentage of a doomed stock can be tied up by those with vested interests (top management comes to mind), and those people are often too steeped in denial to sell. The capper is that companies with depressed share prices can on occasion become takeover candidates, yet another excuse folks conjure up to hold on. Soon after I panned Lomas Financial, the stock leapt 20 percent in one farcical trading session, from $7^{1}/_2$ to 9, on a takeover rumor. But as time wore on, the bad-is-bad principle won out, as there could be no reversing the jam that Lomas had gotten itself into. So please don't tell me that the market was being efficient.

One area in which the market *is* reasonably efficient is within a closely watched industry. With drug stocks, for example, you can be virtually certain that the company with the most exciting new-product portfolio will have a higher price/earnings ratio than the company whose top drugs are about to lose their patent production (a phenomenon that opens the door for generic drug manufacturers to come in at far lower price points). The reason these efficiencies exist is that most major industries are under constant scrutiny by dozens of top-flight analysts who on balance do an excellent job with the basic pecking order of their companies' fundamentals.

However, it is much, much harder for the market to be efficient when it comes to setting price standards between *different* industries, different countries, and so on. One laughable aspect of the efficient market theory is that it has existed in the minds of market academicians for decades—before and during times when many foreign stock markets were categorically out of sync. If those markets were so damned efficient, then how did John Templeton and his billion dollars find an early retirement in Lyford Cay?

Perhaps the market is more efficient today than it was 15 years ago, but so what? You can still make money in drug stocks despite the industry's apparently efficient pricing. Warner-Lambert was seemingly efficiently priced at $30 in 1994. Four years and several impressive new drug releases later, it had soared past $200.

Furthermore, there is a gigantic barrier to the attainment of a truly efficient market, namely, the fact that there are just too many stocks for us to keep track of. Exciting stories fall through the cracks with every passing day. Even though there are more active investors than ever before to monitor the market, with this population explosion comes more and more people who haven't kept up-to-date with any particular stock. If the *Wall Street Journal* makes some positive comments about a company *based solely on already available information,* there will always be those to whom the information is new, and they'll be pushing the stock up as soon as the market opens.

The reason why it is so important to decry the efficient market theory is the widespread abuse that the EMT creates among inexperienced investors: namely, that there is no advantage in doing research simply because everyone else is doing the same thing. By that reckoning, a professional sports team needn't worry about physical conditioning—after all, everybody else is doing the same thing. Conditioning taskmaster Pat Riley found a simple way to express what every EMT abuser should keep in mind: "Being in shape doesn't *guarantee* you anything . . . but without it you don't stand a chance."

In sum, the stock market is neither crazy nor efficient. I will concede that it needn't be fair, and it certainly needn't be right. There can be plenty of luck involved, especially in the short term. But that's where we must part ways with the efficient market theorists. Our goal is to create a long-term advantage by understanding the role of psychology, and there is no reason in the world why that goal cannot be achieved.

WHY RESEARCH ISN'T ENOUGH

Having decried those misapprehensions that cause investors to go easy on their fundamental research, it's time for me to set the stage for the rest of the book by claiming that research alone is not enough. Basic company analysis is the be-all but *not* the end-all of investing in common stocks.

The reason behind this claim is that we are human beings first and investors second. In this section we're going to examine a few syndromes that the average investor faces before, during, and beyond the decision-making process. Some might be foreign to you, but others will be all too familiar. The net effect of these syndromes is that human nature casts an enormous shadow on the entire investment process. And as the first two syndromes demonstrate, psychology can play a decisive role before the research ever begins.

The Implanted Idea

We all get funny ideas in our heads from time to time, and before penning another word I should stress that I'm no exception. Here is a true confession away from the investing world:

Have you ever gotten a song lyric wrong? Not as many times as I have. I thought Aimee Mann (of Til' Tuesday fame) was singing "Hush,

hush, even downtown, voices carry," when in fact the lyrics were "Hush, hush, keep it down now, voices carry." Even worse, I thought Linda Ronstadt (then of the Stone Poneys) started a "Different Drum" passage with "We're both doing our laundry," when in fact she was singing "We'll both live a lot longer . . . if you live without me." Did you notice that in each case the actual lyrics have the advantage of *making sense?*

The problem is that once an off-the-wall notion gets implanted in our heads, any lack of sense the notion may have is irrelevant because by definition it never gets investigated. With song lyrics, there may come a day when we get set straight—ideally not while performing for the queen. In investments, however, the implanted ideas typically go on and on until we pay a price, as in this sad story: In the rocky market year of 1994, one of my top recommendations was Scott Paper, now part of Kimberly-Clark. The reason for my interest was that Scott was just beginning a major cost-cutting program, and the odds seemed high that a more streamlined and profitable company would emerge. Yet one particular couple was dubious. They had met Scott's chief executive officer (CEO) at a Montana dude ranch and had apparently found him quite underwhelming.

The dude ranch story was perplexing to me, inasmuch as Scott's new CEO Al Dunlap was a confirmed workaholic and most unlikely to be spending any of his first year on the job riding horseback. In fact, Dunlap's insatiable appetite for corporate cost-cutting was at the root of my recommendation. Was I missing something? (Please cut me some slack regarding Al Dunlap. His debacle with Sunbeam had yet to occur.) Anyway, only later did I find out that the fateful Montana meeting had taken place in *1962.* Yet its impact was powerful enough to cause this couple to miss a 200 percent gain in Scott shares between the summer of 1994 and the end of 1995, when the sale to Kimberly-Clark concluded Dunlap's whirlwind tenure.

Hapless tales such as this get played out every day. I can count dozens of investors in Boston alone whose antipathy toward Bill Gates made them unable to objectively analyze the treasure chest known as

Microsoft. Meanwhile, thousands of Macintosh users across the country couldn't separate their devotion to their "superior" machines from the sagging fortunes of the company that produced them. As these words were written in 1998, shares of Apple Computer traded lower than they did in 1986. The point is that all the great research in the world isn't worth anything if you're barking up the wrong tree.

Before you say, "Good investors wouldn't make these mistakes," let me assure you that there isn't a professional investor alive who hasn't been hurt by a similar blind spot. As Gillette soared to its umpteenth record high in early 1998, the well-known hedge fund manager Jim Cramer exclaimed, "For just a moment, a brief second today, right about when I was about to shave, I was overcome by my hatred of Gillette." (Hence the goatee?) Well, in Cramer's defense, some of his aversion was well placed: As he said at the time, "Gillette sells at 40 times earnings and has flat sales growth. Did you hear me?" So there was more than mere psychology behind his stance, and before long he would be vindicated. But how far back did his distaste go? The only way that stocks become overpriced is by going up a lot, and one suspects that Cramer wasn't along for Gillette's long ride.

Where the stock market is concerned, we develop mental blocks for a very good reason, and that's the pure size of the investment universe. Without some type of screening mechanism, we might feel totally lost as we confronted the 10,000 or more public companies now cluttering the financial pages. What I intend to encourage in this book is for each of us to develop a *rational* screening process instead of the bias-laden filter of implanted ideas that we might otherwise develop.

Scarcity of Time and Opportunity

One of the most important limitations that part-time investors encounter with their research activities is time itself. Whereas professionals can afford to spend all day investigating a potential investment and deciding *not* to invest, most individuals don't have that luxury.

Isn't it time to acknowledge that many, many individual investors have already decided to buy a stock *before* they ever sit down to analyze it? New ideas don't come along every day, and it is all too easy to tailor information to conform with the thrust of a bullish hypothesis or tip. Truly objective research can be as scarce as a nonpartisan reaction to a convention speech.

I am reminded of Andrew Tobias's wonderful early 1980s tale about a friend who called excitedly with news (mistaken, as it turned out) that Allied Corporation was going to bid $85 per share for 27 percent of Bendix—this for a $57 stock that was already ballooning with takeover speculation. Whether this tidbit constituted inside information is beside the point; Tobias rightly cautioned that an offer for only a percentage of the company would be a disappointment that would push the stock *down*. The friend was momentarily caught off guard but soon came up with an ultraflexible response. "Okay, let's short it then." The story ended in disaster because Allied Corporation, in fact, bid for all of Bendix and the stock jumped up 17 points right after the short had been put in place. So why didn't our friend (or, to be more accurate, Andrew Tobias's friend) simply leave well enough alone? Because for many investors an *opportunity cost*—the official term for the money you *didn't* make on a stock—feels every bit as bad as a loss.

Yes, professionals will tell you you're being silly if you don't distinguish between opportunity costs and actual losses, but there is a fine line between them. Would a baseball manager ever blurt out, "Hey, I don't care that we failed to score after loading the bases in the top of the ninth. We're still up one run"? Of course not. I'm not recommending that investors flog themselves every time they miss a winning stock, but I am suggesting that (1) opportunities don't come around every day and (2) a psychic cost should never be given a value of zero. When professional investors say otherwise, it only proves they've been spending too much time immersed in spreadsheets and not enough time mingling with their own species.

The bottom line is that it goes against human nature to find some titillating information and do nothing. And if our investment program requires that we stop experiencing human nature, we could be in for some very uncomfortable times. Creating the proper balance between recklessness and gratification is a goal worth understanding and pursuing.

Perils of the Buying Moment

Personalities not only affect our universe of eligible investments, they also play a decisive role at the all-important moment of purchase. What follows is an especially thorny issue for the unsuspecting investor, one that adds a new wrinkle to the theoretical preeminence of first-rate research.

Do you own shares of Disney? Microsoft? Fannie Mae? Merck? Gillette? Well, why not? It's hard to take issue with the fact that these are superior companies and in fact they've been that way for a long time. That's what any half-serious research would show, and it's not as if these companies are obscure. Looking back, one could argue that any point in the past 10 years offered a terrific buying opportunity in these stocks. For some of them it's more like 20 years.

Ah, but on what day do you actually pick up the phone and call your broker? There is a paradox in all of this: The cold logic of fundamental analysis notwithstanding, there can be a gigantic gap between those companies whose fundamentals we know to be outstanding and those companies that actually make it into our portfolios.

In an effort to explain this paradox, I came up with a phenomenon that I dubbed "acceptance," which works as follows: When we don't latch onto a success story early on (otherwise the problem doesn't apply), it is all too natural to *accept* the fact that we don't own the stock, whether it be Disney or Fannie Mae or whatever. We smile and say, "You can't win 'em all"—at which point our nonownership becomes a subconscious part of our daily equilibrium, a balance that we as human beings are notoriously reluctant to tinker with. The shame of this whole process, of course, is that a company can go on being successful long after we first rued not buying it.

A significant corollary of the acceptance principle is that arithmetic and emotions can diverge: It is only marginally more painful to miss a stock that's gone up sixfold than to miss one that's merely doubled. This skewing effect is why psychologists might describe *acceptance* as a "maladaptive defense." Whatever the name, we should remember that beating the market is a purely arithmetical goal, so we are well advised to identify these divergences when they occur.

There is another poorly understood yet vitally important issue that relates to the moment of purchase. I'll state it as follows: The act of buying and selling stocks isn't nearly as satisfying as is popularly believed.

Microsoft, for example, is a stock that I first recommended in late 1988. Looking at what's happened to it since, you'd think that the moment of purchase was a tremendously satisfying event, as in, "Bursting with enthusiasm, the young analyst confidently made his case for Microsoft, a once-in-a-lifetime opportunity in the increasingly vital computer software industry." More headlines that never made it into print.

What I was actually thinking at the time of my initial, tepid recommendation was what an idiot I was for not acting *sooner*. By late 1988, Microsoft shares were worth eight times their value at their public offering just two years earlier. Being ever so aware of that price movement, it was impossible for me to act like the purveyor of an original idea—which Microsoft wasn't. Its utter unoriginality grated on me to the point where I almost never mentioned the stock at all. But as an investment columnist I was lucky: I had to write *something*. And Microsoft worked out just fine. If I wasn't writing this book under the influence of truth serum, I'd say I saw the whole thing coming.

When it comes to doling out satisfaction, selling is even stingier than buying. Whereas we needn't be encumbered by the past when we buy a stock, we inevitably encounter psychological issues when we contemplate getting rid of one.

A few years ago I came across a nicely reasoned sell recommendation of CML Group (of NordicTrack fame), written by top-flight analyst
Skip Wells of Adams, Harkness, & Hill. CML's problem was that Nordic-
Track's heyday was over and the other main subsidiary (garden supply
company Smith & Hawken) was unable to take up the slack. CML, at $9,
had been "sent to jail," to use Wells's term. But if you understood his
personal history with the stock—which included riding it up for some
wonderful gains from 1989 to 1991 but then riding it down from its
peak of $30—you knew how wrenching the entire experience must have
been for him. Think about it: On what day do you walk into your office and tell all your clients how wrong you had been for the prior year?
Recommending a sale at a lower price in a sense confirms that you were
even *more* wrong to begin with. Personally, I admired the courage hidden between the lines of his sell recommendation. And later I was able
to admire its accuracy as well. Within four years of Wells's sell recommendation, CML had dropped to below $1 per share.

So the good news is that there is satisfaction in the stock market.
There can be plenty of it, at that. But don't avoid investment moves
just because they don't feel great at the moment of action. Satisfaction,
like practically everything else in the market, can take time.

Discreditation

Our final syndrome kicks in after we've taken investment action. By
the phenomenon of "discreditation" I am referring to the fact that even
the most impeccably reasoned decisions can be near-term disasters, and
there is nothing in the textbooks that prepares the investor for this
nasty experience.

Consider Polaroid and Avon Products, two stocks that hit extraordinary peaks in the giddy market climate of 1972. I can't tell you how
many times I've read about the factors that made these stocks such obvious sale candidates way back then. Polaroid and Avon have been
written about so much because (1) both stocks went down awfully far,

awfully fast, (2) there was ample evidence at the top that a big decline was in store, which leads to (3) the stocks are wonderful models that can be kept in mind for future sell decisions.

Here's the background. Both stocks were charter members of the so-called "Nifty Fifty," the then-cute but now ridiculed coinage for an elite group of institutionally favored buy-and-hold stocks that seemed to assure infinite prosperity. Polaroid shares were trading at 50 times earnings in 1972; Avon was trading at 64 times earnings. Not only were these valuations ludicrous on their face, there weren't enough housewives in America or picture-takers in the free world to support multiples that high. And what happened in the two years that followed was devastating. Between 1972 and 1974, Polaroid tumbled from a high of 143 all the way down to 14; Avon from 140 to 18. The lofty levels of 1972 remained unattainable for years to come.

The problem with using these stocks as your canonical lesson of when to sell lies with the storytelling itself. In order to make the drops of these stocks look as precipitous as possible, the stories typically start at the peak, which is a much different view than the investor has at the time the stock market action is actually being created.

Suppose you had owned Avon in, say, mid-1970, when it was trading at about *$70 per share*. Using the identical argument as before, this was one seriously overpriced stock. It declined 80 percent in the next four years, didn't it? But if you acted on that justifiably bearish view, you would have been forced to look on as the market showed a sickening disregard, pushing Avon shares to two times what you deemed an absurd level. *Viewing this type of market behavior is not fun.* By the time the seller at 70 saw Avon at 140, his or her bearish viewpoint, although utterly sound, would also have been utterly discredited—hence the title of this section.

The illusion persists that there was a moment when you could have concluded that Polaroid and Avon were overpriced, acted on that conclusion, and then sat back to reap your reward while everyone else suffered. But it wasn't so then, and it needn't be so in the future. However immaculate your research, you might well have to contend with a market that refuses to share your pessimism.

This last example by no means minimizes the role of research; on the contrary, it is the well-informed investor who will survive the best when the market is going the wrong way. Discreditation can be temporary, and redemption can take its place. Yet the net effect of all of the syndromes we've just discussed is that the complete investor is more than a mere analyst. The complete investor is one who understands the psychological makeup of the marketplace and who can use that knowledge to leave the competition behind.

CONTRADICTORY ADVICE TO END ALL CONTRADICTORY ADVICE

In the chapters that follow, I'll be dissecting various personality types, one at a time. In preparation, I should mention one teensy-weensy wrinkle of the next chapter that you'll surely notice: The advice won't be consistent.

Sounds odd, doesn't it? After all, a stock that goes up for me will surely go up for you. Yet it's time for investment advice to do a better job of recognizing the individual, because our circumstances and problems are all different. Obese people should eat less. Anorexics should eat more. Alcoholics should drink less. Teetotalers should, well, you get the idea.

I should acknowledge that any portfolio manager worth his or her salt does make an effort to understand a client's basic individual circumstances, including factors such as income requirements and risk tolerances. However, those of us who go it alone must sift through bushels of written and televised advice that purports to be "one size fits all" but that leads to the bewildering and annoying conclusion that the experts often disagree. And I'm not talking about the daily type of disagreement that brings people together to make markets. I'm talking about printed advice, where it can be extremely disconcerting to see one "expert" (time to bring in the quotation marks) recommend the practice of selling a stock after it has gone up 50 percent, only to see another "expert" recommend selling after a stock has gone *down* 20 percent. A new investor may quite reasonably ask what in the world is going on. The following is my attempt at a simple explanation.

If you're wondering who the people are that recommend selling after a 50 percent gain, the most frequently cited advocate is none other than Benjamin Graham—as in the coauthor (with David Dodd) of the classic book *Security Analysis;* as in the sobriquet "the father of fundamental analysis"; as in the mentor of Warren Buffett. With credentials such as these, we are well advised to listen.

What has to be understood, though, is that Graham's sell discipline evolved as the logical companion to a very specific purchase strategy. What Graham recognized many decades ago was that the stock market sometimes forgetfully pushed companies to such a low level that their entire market capitalization was less than what he termed their "net current assets," defined as current assets minus total liabilities. In other words, the ongoing businesses of these companies were given a value of *zero*. Graham didn't actually care what these companies did, but he reckoned that most of the businesses were worth *something*; he therefore held three years or until the stock had gone up 50 percent, whichever came first. The 50 percent figure was somewhat arbitrary, but it proved both realistic and profitable. Once attained, Graham would sell the stock and invest in something else that happened to satisfy his original purchase criteria. And if the stock didn't move in three years, well, nobody's perfect.

Dr. Martin Zweig, author of *The Zweig Forecast* and *Winning on Wall Street,* has lived by a very different set of rules. He will almost automatically get out of a stock if it goes down 20 percent, sometimes through the mechanism of a *stop-loss order,* which is basically an instruction to the broker to sell if the stock hits the predetermined loss trigger (15 percent, 20 percent, or whatever). Many if not most traders and technical analysts follow this same pattern. Their objective is to make money by latching on to popular stocks and riding the positive momentum. The idea is that even a success ratio as low as 60 percent can lead to tremendous performance, as long as the gains from the winners exceed the losses from the losers. Maintaining a price-sensitive sell discipline helps to achieve that outcome.

Now, one of these strategies may be of far greater personal appeal to you than the other, but no matter; the point is that the two selling strategies are so different because the underlying *purchase* strategies are so different. You can be certain that Ben Graham didn't have to fight off any momentum investors to establish his positions, and vice versa. Nonetheless, these conflicting bits of advice land on our heads without any sort of reconciling backdrop. Quite a shame, because there is nothing more frustrating or unprofitable for the new investor than to accidentally merge two conflicting strategies. Investing in the stock market can be extremely dangerous when done à la carte.

If you think you can avoid this destructive mismatching simply through the route of long-term investing, guess again. It is vital to understand that an individual company can drastically change its investment stripes in even a few short years, thereby wreaking havoc with a conventionally tailored investment plan. The company I've chosen to illustrate this is Callaway Golf, pioneers of the Big Bertha golf club. The company went public in 1992. Here's what happened in the six years that followed. (See chart on page 22.)

Six intervals stand out:

1. *The flip.* Some of the early Callaway investors participated for only a matter of hours. In the company's very first day of trading (fittingly, February 29, the leap day), the stock jumped from the $20 offering price all the way to $36, a gain of 80 percent. This gain is now totally obscured by the long-term price chart—which also includes the three stock splits enacted by Callaway over the years—but it was very real at the time.

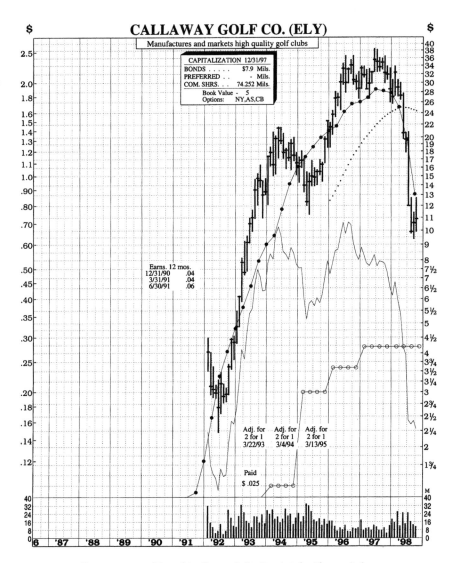

CALLAWAY GOLF CO. (ELY)

Manufactures and markets high quality golf clubs

CAPITALIZATION 12/31/97
BONDS . . . . . $7.9 Mils.
PREFERRED . .   - Mils.
COM. SHRS. . .   74.252 Mils.
Book Value -   5
Options: NY,AS,CB

Earns. 12 mos.
12/31/90   .04
3/31/91   .04
6/30/91   .06

Adj. for   Adj. for   Adj. for
2 for 1   2 for 1   2 for 1
3/22/93   3/4/94   3/13/95

Paid
$ .025

Chart courtesy of Securities Research Co. Reprinted with permission.

2. *IPO backlash.* Unfortunately, the more "flippers" that participate in an initial public offering (IPO), the more unstable the
stock price tends to be. Within four months of the offering, the
stock had dropped 50 percent from its high. Callaway investors
at that time had to deal with snickering from all directions about
the priciness of the stock and the inherent riskiness of IPOs. Ultimately, they had to decide whether they still wanted to participate in a perverse arena where short-term return on investment
can shrink as corporate performance skyrockets.

3. *Glory days.* Once the IPO hangover subsides, fortunes can be
made: in this case, up 10-fold in two years. Momentum investors
love situations like this. Don't we all love to make 900 percent
on our money? Well, after the fact, yes, but keep in mind that
holding the stock throughout this time, while requiring no physical effort, wasn't the easiest decision in the world. The enemy
was that inner voice crying out that the good times couldn't possibly last, a perception that for some people tainted the stock
even in early 1993—never mind that there was plenty of upside
remaining.

4. *Comeuppance.* Every company has its time of reckoning, and
Callaway's finally came in 1994. The year started brightly—in
fact, earnings rose almost 80 percent for the year—but investors
were already looking ahead to a softer 1995, in which earnings
would increase "only" 30 percent. This is the type of short-term
disappointment that the market rarely tolerates. Momentum investors were now through for good, short-sellers were having
their day in the sun, and it remained to be seen whether the
company could recover.

5. *Rebound.* In mid-1995, arguably for the first time, Callaway
gained some appeal as a *value* investment. Typically, value investors start to move into a stock only after the momentum players are all out—in fact, it is the very exodus of the momentum

investors that helps create the value! At $11 per share, a paltry 10 times trailing earnings, Callaway was now priced to perform. And when earnings moved up strongly for the following two years, the stock followed suit, appreciating 200 percent from its undeserved lows of 1995.

6. *Orient expressed.* In theory, there was no reason why the rebound couldn't keep going, but in fact it didn't. Some investors became frightened by the talk that a tightening of PGA standards could actually outlaw the core of the Callaway line. That didn't happen, but what did happen in 1998 is that the company became a victim of the Asian economic crisis, and any investor who saw the link had an advantage in getting out.

It is no secret that the Japanese love the game of golf, so much so that the island can't accommodate enough courses to satisfy demand, which then spills over to indoor driving ranges and the like. (True story: A friend of mine, while serving as a Japanese/English interpreter for the State Department, lost track of a conversation and was forced to improvise by asking the visitor, "Do you like golf?" knowing that the answer would be affirmative and that the conversation would be given a fresh start, albeit a manipulated one.) Well, when the Japanese economy did its sharp pullback, Callaway's expensive titanium golf clubs were an early casualty. The company eventually released its new and cheaper steel "woods" in the summer of 1998, but by then the stock had backtracked into the midteens, as investors concluded that lower-priced products could result in a permanent downward shift in Callaway's profit margins.

So much for buying a stock and leaving it alone. The most important message from this "Cliff Notes" history is that investment success isn't limited to any one personality type; and if that's true for a single stock, it's emphatically true for the market as a whole. There's room for all of us, as long as we forge a strategy that's consistent with who we are.

In discussing these various strategies, whether they be for contrarians, visionaries, or bargain hunters, my approach will be strictly non-judgmental. As far as I'm concerned, each of the upcoming styles has plusses and minuses, and most of us will find pieces of ourselves in many different categories.

Also in keeping with sound therapeutic practice, my recommendations will follow parallel tracks. On the one hand, I will encourage each group to try and break through the shackles of whatever limited market orientation it happens to live by. On the other hand, I will recognize that at some point we have to acknowledge our limitations and make the most of what comes naturally. Those are the ground rules. Without further ado, let us go on to the main stock market personality types.

"Where is whatever is reduced fifty per cent?"

THE
BARGAIN
HUNTER

If you could own 100 shares of any stock you wanted, which company would you choose? Trick question. The answer is Berkshire Hathaway, which has been known to hover north of $60,000 per share.

If that particular price tag scares you off, take heart. There is a bit of a bargain hunter in everyone. Well, almost everyone. You've probably met people who simply have to own the most expensive item they can, whether it be a car, a dining room table, or a bathing suit. But even these folks change their ways when it comes to the stock market. Unless we are handed a bunch of shares, as in the conjured-up example above, none of us invests by seeking out the most expensive stocks.

Of course, it doesn't take long for new investors to realize that the absolute price of a stock ($30, $150, or even $60,000) isn't what defines a bargain or a rip-off. The stock's price relative to the company's earnings

ARE YOU A BARGAIN HUNTER?

Answer these questions and find out:

1 If you're on your way to—(Broadway play, Daytona 500, church) and you see a sign for a garage sale, do you pull over?

Axiomatic.

2 Would you rather buy a $1,000 suit for $500 or a $200 suit for $200?

If you're in the first group, you just might be a bargain hunter. If you're in the second group, you just might be cheap. There's a big difference. Bargain hunters have a much better shot at stock market stardom.

3 Do you lean toward stocks that are at the low end of their 52-week trading range?

It is comforting for bargain hunters to know that the price they paid was the best price they could have realistically gotten. If someone else got it much cheaper a few months before, some of the luster is gone.

4 Do you ask your friends how much they paid for certain acquisitions?

As we will see in the chapter, it is possible to carry this practice too far.

5 Have you ever been called an insecure narcissist?

Odds are you haven't, but that's a general description of the anti-bargain hunter—someone who simply must have the most expensive item in any setting, from an auction to a restaurant. If you're in that category, this chapter might not be a very good fit.

is what matters, which is why the world needs a *price/earnings ratio*. A $150 stock price on a company that is earning $10 per share translates into a price/earnings ratio, or P/E, of 15. Similarly, a $30 stock price on a company that is earning $1.25 per share translates into a P/E of 24. The $30 stock is thus "more expensive" than the $150 stock. You may have been told once upon a time that price/earnings ratios were complex. Now you know better.

The one teensy-weensy complication lies in defining a P/E for the overall market. This construction requires creating a composite earnings figure for the average itself, which consists of 30 companies for the Dow Jones Industrial Average or 500 companies for the Standard & Poor's (S&P) 500. It's messy, but suffice it to say that people have figured out how to do it. A bargain hunter will then automatically gravitate toward stocks whose P/E is lower than that of the overall market. If successful investing were that simple, this chapter would end right here. But as you can see, we're only beginning.

BRIGHT SPOTS

The ideal scenario for a bargain hunter is a "double play" of higher earnings and higher valuation, which works as follows: You find a stock selling for a below-market multiple—say, 10 times earnings—at a time when the overall market is selling for 15 times earnings. Now suppose the company in question performs well and maintains a 12 percent growth rate. Five years down the road, earnings will be 76 percent higher (not 60 percent higher—that's the beauty of compounded growth*). The double play is that the stock should be even more than 76 percent higher, assuming that the market rewards the company's

---

* If earnings are increasing by 12 percent a year, they are being multiplied by a factor of 1.12 each year. After five years, earnings will have gone up by a factor of $1.12 \times 1.12 \times 1.12 \times 1.12 \times 1.12$, or 1.76, which corresponds to a 76 percent increase.

sustained earnings growth with a higher multiple. If the multiple goes up from 10 to 14, your total return on the stock will be $76 \times 1.4 = 106$ percent. Not too shabby for an investment that is by its nature conservative. Throw in some dividend income and the total return picture gets even brighter.

The numbers in the prior example were made up, but I should emphasize that the market can be even more generous in real life. I remember stumbling across a surprise bonanza in the spring of 1991 while writing a regular column called "Uncommon Stocks" for Fidelity's *Investment Vision* magazine. The subject of my April column was the defense industry, then enjoying a rare moment of public affection following America's success in the Persian Gulf. Valuation was an important part of the investment equation: at the time, defense stocks were trading at an average of eight times earnings, only half the multiple accorded the overall market. Were things really that bad?

Looking through the rearview mirror, there was no shortage of concerns. Following the defense boom of the early Reagan years, legislators had taken aim at the defense industry throughout the 1980s. The installation of fixed-price contracts cut the fat out of defense budgets; a reduction in federal progress payments forced defense contractors to put up more of their own money to see a project through to completion; the 1986 tax-law changes effectively accelerated the tax liability on long-term contracts. However, the industry remained profitable, and the visible triumph in the Persian Gulf figured to reverse the austere legislative environment and the pessimistic investment climate that went with it. Within a few short years, stocks such as Raytheon and General Dynamics had moved up 80 percent and *240* percent, respectively, far outpacing the overall market. And the merger mania that forged Martin Marietta into Lockheed and McDonnell Douglas into Boeing also made for some very happy shareholders.

Did I see all of this coming? In a word, no. All I saw were cheap stocks with turnaround potential, not table-pounding buys. The "buying moment" hurdles I alluded to in the introduction stand especially tall for value-oriented investments because low P/E stocks, by definition, will never include the snazziest growth stories the country has to offer. If you need excitement to justify a purchase, you'd never have bought these stocks.

Speaking of "buying moment blahs," later that same year I wrote an article entitled "Changing Stripes," which focused on a timeless source of opportunity in the low P/E realm: the company undergoing a fundamental change in identity. The idea is to take advantage of long-standing negative investor perceptions of a company in hopes that the market will accord the "new and improved" version a higher multiple. At that time, Hasbro (making acquisitions to smooth out its earnings stream), Dial (sloughing off its misfit Greyhound bus lines), and Briggs & Stratton (finally producing engines cheaply) all fit the bill. And the strategy worked like a charm. Hasbro shares were up 100 percent in two years. Dial, net of its divestitures, was up 80 percent. Briggs & Stratton doubled its profit margins within four years and saw its share price triple, a welcome change from years of aimlessness. (See chart on page 32.)

Again, I have to admit that these stocks lacked pizazz. If you had asked me the day after I wrote the "Changing Stripes" article whether I had any *hot* new ideas, I'd have had to say no. As a financial writer, I had the advantage of being forced to come up with something to fill the page, and I thought these ideas made sense. But only the person whose pulse thrived on finding a bargain would have even glanced at the article, much less bought the stocks.

PITFALLS

Having dredged out my personal highlight film of bargain hunting ideas, let me confess that it is indeed possible to take the strategy too

Chart courtesy of Securities Research Co. Reprinted with permission.

far. In real life the symptoms of excess bargain hunting are easy to detect. I accidentally developed my own rule back in 1985 when I became the proud owner of two Siberian Husky puppies. The certifiable bargain hunters were the ones who were willing to toe the line of tackiness by asking me how much the puppies had cost.

I know—there are any number of legitimate reasons why someone might have been curious about the sticker price of my new sled team. But there are also at least two good reasons why the question was a silly one. The obvious rebuttal was the fact that these animals would pay back the initial investment 1,000-fold by their very being. But even just looking at dollars and cents, when you've signed on for 12-plus years of heartworm pills, rabies shots, springtime groomings, and enough dry dog food to fill Lake Huron, the purchase price doesn't begin to tell the whole story. I won't push the analogy too far, but I will say that bargain hunters on Wall Street can err in two respects: (1) they can miss out altogether, or (2) they can be wrongly lured by a low purchase price.

When Low P/Es Are a Red Flag

The biggest challenge facing value-oriented investors is that plenty of low P/E stocks have earned their low valuations through downright mediocrity. Weeding out the chaff is a difficult task for any investor, and all the more so when you've chosen the most chaff-filled subsector the stock market has to offer. All in all, I'd rather delve into a bunch of good companies and pick the cheapest one rather than delve into a bunch of cheap stocks and try to find the best one.

One common trap for the unwary bargain hunter is found among cyclical companies. A cyclical company, in contrast to a growth company, is one whose earnings go up and down with the economic cycle. Macroeconomic cycles can be vague, but many cyclical companies are more readily analyzed because they move in conjunction with the price

of a specific commodity, such as oil, steel, or even gold. When investing in the stocks of commodity producers, the whole idea is to catch the
early upward move in the commodity price. The game is a dangerous
one, however, because these stocks typically peak well before the actual
commodity price reversal. For our present purposes, the important point
is that the peak is attained at a time when earnings are strong, meaning that *P/Es at cyclical peaks can be extremely low.* Hence the trap.

The Methanex saga illustrates this phenomenon beautifully. The
company produces methanol, which, in case you've missed the annual
reports, is a "primary liquid petrochemical made from fossil fuels con-
taining carbon and hydrogen." As the accompanying table shows,
Methanex lost $9 million on sales of $116 million in 1992, and its stock
traded for about $6 per share. Nothing very interesting so far. Late that
year, however, a windfall appeared in the form of an amendment to the
Clean Air Act. The amendment mandated that gasolines in some 23
states maintain a minimum percentage of so-called "oxygenated fuels."
This stipulation basically referred to MTBE (methyl tertiary butyl ether),
of which methanol was the main ingredient. So much for the scientific
jargon. The point is that the newfound demand for methanol pushed
prices sharply higher. Methanex's revenues for 1993 came in at a cool
$533 million, by far the highest in the company's history.

In 1994, things got even better. Methanex became the beneficiary of
some freak shutdowns at several competitors' plants, and the resulting

The Methanex Boom

		1992	1993	1994	1995	1996
Revenues ($mil)		116	533	1488	1249	946
Net income		(9)	11	443	200	(8)
Net profit margin		—	2.0%	29.8%	16.0%	—
Earnings per share		(0.20)	0.06	2.24	1.05	(0.04)
Share price range	High	$10^3/_8$	$9^3/_4$	$18^3/_8$	$15^1/_4$	$10^1/_8$
	Low	$6^3/_8$	$5^1/_2$	$7^3/_4$	6	$6^1/_2$

supply shortage pushed the methanol price higher still. By the fall of 1994, Methanex shares had risen to about $18—three times its level before the boom, but still only seven times the $2.24 per share the company would earn that year. Yet even at that low P/E, the stock was an absolute sale. Not only were the various overseas suppliers racing to rectify their shutdowns, but other companies had announced plans to build new methanol plants. These plants wouldn't be onstream for years to come, but when the laws of supply and demand are rearing their ugly heads (extra supply implies lower prices in the future), there is no point in sticking around. The MTBE boom was a once-in-a-generation phenomenon, and it was over. By 1996 Methanex's boom had become a loss. Its share price had dropped back down to $6, completing a breathtaking round trip. Even two years after that, the company had to contend with a supply overhang caused by the earlier plant construction. Those who understood the precariousness of the earnings pattern would have known to sell the stock. But remember that you had to resist your bargain hunting instincts and sell despite an extremely low P/E.

Although an extended bull market has arguably cut down on the number of bargain hunting opportunities, the actual process of finding stocks with low P/Es has only gotten easier. Nowadays most newspapers include a P/E column in their stock tables, and there are any number of online databases that enable investors to screen for stocks satisfying certain basic pricing criteria. But keep in mind that in almost all cases, these P/E figures are *trailing* figures, meaning that they'll tell you precisely what the company in question earned *last year,* and that's all. If you had seen Methanex at $14 in early 1995, the stock would have seemed quite attractive, statistically. But statistics can lie; and a low trailing P/E is a fibber par excellence.

Consider that the same early 1995 stock screen might have sent you to Northeast discount retailer Caldor, then trading at a paltry seven times trailing earnings. I had looked at the stock the prior year and thought it attractive, based on solid same-store sales growth, a stepped-up schedule for new store openings, and a reasonable valuation. But the company had a disastrous fourth quarter of 1994, and the stock had fallen from a mid-1994 peak of $34 down to about $17. At that point it showed up in a *Wall Street Journal* screen of the cheapest stocks out there, based on 1994 earnings of $2.44 per share. However, the fundamental picture for 1995 was spiraling downward. When Ames, another discount chain, declared bankruptcy early that year, you'd think that would have helped Caldor, but the reverse was true. Suppliers feared that Caldor might suffer the same fate, and by holding back on merchandise that summer they made those fears self-fulfilling. A nasty vicious circle. Time to sell, wouldn't you say?

Believe it or not, many folks were clinging on. Even late in 1995, while I was writing commentaries for America Online's personal finance area, I noticed that many message-board postings were still *positive* toward Caldor because of its low P/E, even though the depletion of the company's cash reserves was by then leading toward almost certain bankruptcy. Having been attuned to the trends earlier in the year, my own experience with the stock wasn't cataclysmic; it was merely dreadful. But the entire episode underscored that a low price/earnings multiple does not provide a safety net. When a company's earnings disappear, any low P/E it might have had during its money-making days is a dangerous illusion. Caldor went out of business for good in 1999.

How Bargain Hunters Can Miss Out

Let's shift gears. To understand precisely how and why a bargain hunter can possibly lose in a game based on finding bargains, you have to understand that the bargain hunter's aversion to high P/Es is based on the following undesirable scenario: Suppose you find a company you'd love to invest in, perhaps because it is growing at the rate of 20 percent per year. However, upon checking the arithmetic, you discover that the stock trades at 30 times earnings. Too high, you say. What you fear is that even if earnings proceed at their brisk pace for the next three years, the multiple may come down to a more realistic 20 times earnings.

Under that assumption, the stock will have appreciated only 15 percent, because the 73 percent gain in earnings will have been counterbalanced by the drop in the earnings multiple.* Three years for a lousy 15 percent isn't worth the trouble.

But experienced stock market participants may have detected a major fallacy in this scenario, one that's worth stating as a general rule to the entire bargain hunting community and beyond: *When a company continues to grow at a healthy clip, its price/earnings multiple rarely shrinks.*

This shrinkage is *possible,* of course, especially in the short term. For proof you need only look back a few years at computer networking pioneer Cisco Systems, whose multiple shrank roughly from 40 to 15 between 1993 and 1994, despite a regular stream of quarterly earnings advances. The market's skittishness was traceable not only to the string of interest rate hikes that plagued 1994 for a wide variety of stocks, but also to the market's decision to penalize Cisco because the company began delivering merely on-target growth, a comedown from its prior pattern of consistently beating the Street's quarterly estimates. The sharp decline in Cisco stock was a gigantic "I told you so" from bargain hunters and, for the moment, was utterly discrediting to many growth-oriented investors.

However, the Cisco exception surely proves the rule because when a company continues to perform well and finds its P/E going down, the stage might well be set for outstanding future performance. From discreditation can spring redemption; and in Cisco's case, three years and many successful acquisitions following the 1994 swoon, the company's earnings had increased by 150 percent and the stock's multiple had swelled to 50 times earnings. This combination made for a gain of over

---

* Suppose the company was earning $1.00 per share at the beginning of the period, with a stock price of $30 (30 times earnings). After three years of 20 percent growth, earnings per share would be $1.73 (1.2 times 1.2 times 1.2 equals 1.728). If the multiple declined to 20 times earnings during this period, the ending stock price would be 20 times $1.73, or $34.60. This amounts to a 15 percent gain over the original price of $30.

700 percent.* And I'm not even cherry-picking my numbers to make the double play look good, because the highs of 1997 were only exceeded when 1998 rolled around.

In fact, when you think of the one-time high-fliers that wound up stumbling in a big way (Boston Chicken, Snapple and even Netscape), you'll almost always find that the decline was based on a serious shortfall in corporate performance, not just a high P/E. Contrary to conventional wisdom, it is unusual for a meaningful decline in a company or an industry to be *purely* price-based.

You'd think I might regret having made that last statement because the markets of 1929, 1972, and 1987 provide an obvious counterargument, as do such industry-specific bubbles as technology in 1983 and biotech in 1991. However, these watershed periods arise infrequently and arguably get more attention than they deserve. Besides, they are surely outnumbered by the occasions in which investors sell stocks because they "feel too high," a notion that is based more on perception than arithmetic. John Rothchild, author of *A Fool and His Money* and *The Bear Book,* laments that years ago he bought a small amount of Berkshire Hathaway at $3,000 per share, only to sell out at $12,000 based on "feels too high" syndrome. The good news is that the stock's subsequent behavior gave him a story to tell. The bad news is that it takes a lot of stories to fill the $60,000 per share void.

GAME PLAN

If you want to be a bargain hunter, you have to be flexible. You cannot cling to any set notion of what constitutes too high a P/E because the benchmark varies with general economic trends. Price/earnings ratios vaulted to new highs in the late 1990s based on a thriving economy and

---

* Trust me on this one.

on lower interest rates, leaving bargain hunters in the dust. I'm not suggesting that you start paying 40 times earnings just because everyone else is doing so; but if your grandfather told you that anything over 10 times earnings was too much, that was then and this is now. I remember Nancy Friday's tale of the woman [herself?] who habitually cut off the ends of the roast before putting it into the oven. When asked why, she replied, "Because my mother did it." When her mother was asked the same question, the reply was also the same: "Because *my* mother did it." The mother's aged mother clarified the entire matter by saying, "My roasting pan was very small. The only way I could fit the meat in it was to cut off the ends."

A flexible bargain hunter should recognize that P/Es only begin to tell the story of whether or not a stock is cheap. A trained seal with a PC can produce lists of stocks with low P/Es, but it takes a true analyst to enlarge the list. Ace bargain hunters Glenn Greenberg and John Shapiro at Chieftain Capital once glommed on to a shipping company called Gotaas-Larsen, whose investment appeal derived from its 20-year leases on several liquefied natural gas (LNG) carriers. The payments on these leases were guaranteed by the Indonesian government, but this steady source of cash was obscured by operating difficulties elsewhere and by the stock market's perception of shipping as a risky business. It took a while for this perception to change, but the result was a 10-fold gain in seven years. Stocks such as these are always out there, but they don't always show up in the low P/E screens.

If you have access to these screens and enjoy the convenience, the last tip I can give is to be on the lookout for opportunities such as the Cisco dip, where the P/E may not be low by market standards, but may represent a bargain basement level relative to sustainable earnings growth. Where stocks are concerned, getting the proverbial $1,000 suit for $500 is much better than getting a $200 suit for $200, which is why the question was included in the quiz that launched this chapter. As long as your holdings increase in value, they are retroactive bargains, which is the very best type of all.

Each of our chapters will have a personality spotlight, in which we look at adjectives and/or attributes that are somehow related (perhaps not at first glance) to the personality type we are talking about. Our spotlight for the bargain hunter may come as something of a surprise.

 # Personality Spotlight

Tidiness

The reason that tidiness enters the picture is that for many bargain hunters, the use of price/earnings ratios or even book values is an attempt to instill some order into an otherwise chaotic world of investments. That attempt is futile, of course, just as we will find the skeptic's pursuit of perfection to be futile. Yet once you identify that the need for order plays a role in the formation of an investment strategy, you may find it easier to overcome this weakness of the bargain hunter approach.

If it's tidiness you're after, you can achieve it by keeping immaculate files of your trades, account statements, annual reports, and any other investment-related paraphernalia. You can maintain online files and produce your own regular printouts of your account's performance, knowing your net assets at every point along the way.

This is all stupid stuff, you might say, but what we're trying to address is a bargain hunter's fundamental discomfort with a stock that's trading at 30 times earnings, given that the P/E could just as easily be at 25 or 35, depending on the whim of the market. That lack of precision is, well, untidy, but that's the way things go. It's true that there is more fluff in the P/E of a single moment than many of us would like, but we are well advised to live with that imprecision in the hopes that the longer-term P/E will move in accordance with the company's growth. In the meantime, we have to generate whatever tidiness we need because we cannot depend on the market to do so.

It was JFK who said, "If we cannot end our differences, we can at least make the world safe for diversity." When you boil this global rhetoric down to personality quirks, it means that we have to develop strategies that enable us either to eliminate those quirks or to live peacefully with them. If you've guessed that we'll be spending a lot of time with the latter option, you guessed right.

"Maw! Myrtle's back. Looks like she made good."

THE
VISIONARY

I have to admit, I wish I were a visionary. I wish I had the Jobsian vision of a computer on every desk or Ray Kroc's vision of a McDonald's in every town in America. That's a real talent. Not everyone has it, and I'm jealous as hell of those who do.

The key unspoken word here is *change*. Humans are not programmed to like change. We thrive on security and familiarity. The biggest change of all is called death, and we hate the very thought of that one.

Visionaries cultivate change, and I'm not exactly sure how they pull it off. I've heard theories that they are motivated by childhood unhappiness, in that it's easy to seek change if you don't like the hand you were originally dealt. But we could probably uncover childhood discontent in all 6 billion residents of planet Earth if we had the time. If the visionaries hadn't been so successful, we'd never be scouring their pasts for the magic ingredients.

So how do you know when you have that magic ingredient of vision? There are certainly different levels of the game. On the top level

43

ARE YOU A VISIONARY?

Answer these questions and find out:

1 Do you have children?

> *Sorry, but a "yes" answer does not automatically qualify you as a visionary. However, the experience of raising a child creates an important mindset wherein the imperfections of any particular day can be tolerated as long as the forward-going picture is still bright.*

2 Did you have a contented childhood?

> *Nothing wrong with being content. However, visions are concocted out of what might be, not what is, and the perverse result is that the contented can be at a disadvantage.*

3 Do you know how the market closed yesterday?

> *Visionaries don't always care about that sort of thing.*

4 "I dream things that never were, and ask 'Why not?'" Does that describe you?

> *The quote is, of course, from Bobby Kennedy, via Rudyard Kipling. A hackneyed phrase, but one that listeners inevitably match against their own personal history. If you want the visionary label, you can't afford to come up short.*

5 Are you absentminded?

> *Visionaries get so focused on their specific goal that they can become remarkably absentminded when it comes to just about anything else.*

would be the likes of Walt Disney, who was able to transform a bunch of orange groves into the world's most popular theme park. The second, more practical level would include such groups as architects, television programmers, and baseball scouts, to whom projecting into the future is an everyday event. For the rest of us, I have devised a simple test. Go back to the first time you heard "Tie a Yellow Ribbon 'Round the Ole Oak Tree," circa 1973. If you foresaw that you'd be hearing the same song in the produce aisle 25 years later, you may have vision after all.

I'm not really joking. Vision is that special imagination capable of extracting meaningful possibilities from apparent nothingness. Practitioners of the art are always looking ahead to what might be, never settling for what is. When you gear your mind to the future in this fashion, the world becomes a different place. And so does the stock market.

BRIGHT SPOTS

The investment advantage held by visionaries can be astounding because they above all others are willing to look beyond Wall Street's quarterly obsessions and see a true winner in the making. The potential winners we're talking about are growth stocks, which with few exceptions are distinct from the bargain hunting stocks we encountered in the preceding chapter. Most of these companies begin life as a concept and spend years hammering that concept into reality.

One subtle item in the investor's favor is that the visionary company is public in the first place. Being short of capital is the great killer of new ideas, and companies that have been able to raise money via a public offering are two steps ahead of the game. Sam Walton was in deep financial trouble in the early days of Wal-Mart, and it was only begrudgingly that he agreed to sell shares to the public. But sell he did, and everyone gained in the process.

The great visionary investments have two primary features: the first is a powerful idea, the second is execution. There are hundreds of companies that have satisfied that one-two punch over the years, and Wal-Mart is certainly one of the most prominent. But if I had to pick one stock that exemplified visionary investing in the 1990s, it would be America Online. As it turns out, the AOL triumph highlights many distinct characteristics that an investor should be on the lookout for.

See for Yourself

The first point is that if you aren't a visionary, it helps enormously to have firsthand experience with the phenomenon in which you're considering investing. But you have to be careful to separate your own personal experiences from those of the rest of the world. If you will indulge me telling a compact version of my own AOL story, you'll see what I mean.

With AOL, I had a true baptism by fire. My first exposure to the service arose in 1994, when I was called upon to write daily commentaries and manage an online portfolio for the *Worth* magazine online area. It was in some sense a wonderful opportunity, but as a practical matter the setting was unfamiliar and the daily grind was onerous. I began to dread so much as logging on to AOL, much less embracing it. If that deterrent weren't enough, America Online shares were the highlight choice from day one of the Motley Fool, the soon-to-be-renowned online investment service that debuted that year. Surely they understood AOL a whole lot better than I did. Besides, what self-respecting contrarian would bother to follow a company that had been "taken" by someone else?

But soon this contrarian attitude changed. The transforming events were that (1) the magazine and I were unable to agree on a forward-going format for our online work, so we parted ways at the end of the year; and (2) AOL asked me if there were anything else I'd like to try. To their utter surprise, I said I would love to take a sabbatical from financial writing and create an online murder-mystery site. To my utter surprise, they said, "Go for it."

And so it was that in the spring of 1995 I traveled to Vienna for a crash course on the AOL system. Okay, it was Vienna, Virginia, not Vienna, Austria, but even in a Beltway office park, a nonvisionary like me could see that there was something special going on inside. Instant messages were exploding like popcorn on my computer screen. I got one pep talk after another from my new supervisors, who frankly behaved more like colleagues. Community spirit was in the air. CEO Steve Case walked up the stairs in a short-sleeved madras shirt, and about 20 people followed closely behind. When I finally exited the building, the cabbie regaled me with stories of secretaries-turned-millionaires via AOL shares. I couldn't help but laugh, mostly at myself and my wariness of high fliers. Could I have gone to the corporate headquarters of, say, Shoney's and felt the same sort of vibes?

The next year confirmed that emotions run particularly high when it comes to visionary companies. The good will that AOL showed toward me enabled me to churn out some 1,500 pages of short mysteries in twelve months (some sabbatical); but as I ran the mystery site, it became apparent to me that not everyone held AOL in such high esteem. Many subscribers hated having to wait for artwork to download before they could log on; others had slow connections that spoiled all the fun; and *everyone* seemed to dislike the hourly charges they were racking up—the era of flat fees had not yet arrived.

Mind you, all of the above thorns could be categorized under "growing pains," and over time the company addressed each and every one. But many observers let these negatives obscure the sensational underlying growth. By 1998, AOL had been given the ultra-ironic label "the company with 10 million dissatisfied customers"—this for an online service that in 1994 had yet to cross the 1 million mark. The point is that while the ebbs and flows of my personal reactions toward this company might have been understandable, it is essential that those attitudes be thrown away when making an investment decision. The market doesn't care how you feel about a company, and it doesn't care about how I feel. Carrying baggage can only be a hindrance.

Don't Expect Bargains

I've already warned you that growth stocks and value stocks seldom mix. When faced with dynamic growth, investors are sometimes better off throwing away their price/earnings ratios. That's because the market is merely a discounting mechanism, not a visionary, and it is ill-equipped to handle exceptional companies. *Exceptional* is a dangerous word to throw around because not many companies deserve such a lofty designation. But when they do, measuring the stock by a P/E is like taking a ruler to measure Pike's Peak.

Sometimes you don't even have any earnings to deal with, as was the case in the early days of cable television. Because the costs of establishing a nationwide network were so high, earnings were low, and cable companies were best valued by a dollar-per-subscriber figure—based on future cash flow—rather than by a multiple of current earnings. Years later, Internet companies such as Excite and Amazon.com were able to generate tremendous investor enthusiasm despite the absence of current earnings. Ditto for AOL, whose barrage of free disk mailings cost a fortune but also built a franchise. Investing for the future is a legitimate corporate strategy, and whatever the medium, investors with 20-10 vision should be willing to pay up as long as they know how future earnings are going to be generated.

On a different note, even though stocks of fast-growing companies tend to have high P/Es, do *not* infer from this valuation that the market understands the story just as well as you do. A high relative multiple simply indicates that the market is expecting more from this growth company than it expects from blue chips such as General Electric or Minnesota Mining. But just as Newtonian physics broke down at high speeds, conventional P/E ranges are ill-equipped to handle the fastest growing companies in the investment universe. Better yet, it doesn't take an Einstein to make that discovery.

Simple arithmetic is actually a growth-stock investor's secret weapon. Growth is *geometric*—it builds on itself—which is how it can overcome a one-dimensional impediment like a high P/E. You won't always succeed, but the maximum loss on even the most spectacular meltdown is 100 percent, whereas the benefits of compound growth operate without bound. The only psychological requirement for growth-stock investors is the ability to shrug off the inevitable mishap as you pocket your winnings from your successes.

Advantage Big Thinker

The final point about visionary investments is that if you trust the company to do its job properly, the qualitative ways in which you might analyze it can be every bit as valuable as balance-sheet analysis. Knowing that Haloid Xerox held the patent on a revolutionary copying machine was more important than knowing the company's cost of goods sold or accounts receivable. With America Online, an investor had to be able to answer the "big picture" questions that arose along the way: Could AOL actually displace Compuserve as the leader? Yes. Compuserve had the misfortune to own the online position before there *was* an online position, and its unfriendly name and nerdy digital e-mail addresses gave AOL a big advantage—the same type of advantage with which Lotus 1-2-3 had displaced one-time spreadsheet leader Visicalc. Okay, but would Microsoft's new service take over? No. By the time the Microsoft Network arrived, AOL's momentum was firmly established. The final qualitative touch was to understand that the very name "America Online" was an extraordinarily powerful marketing force and, by contrast, made "The Microsoft Network" appear like a corporate division rather than an inspiration. (See chart on page 50.)

All an investor really had to do was believe in the power of a friendly online service and keep the faith that the company's many

AMERICA ONLINE, INC. (AOL)

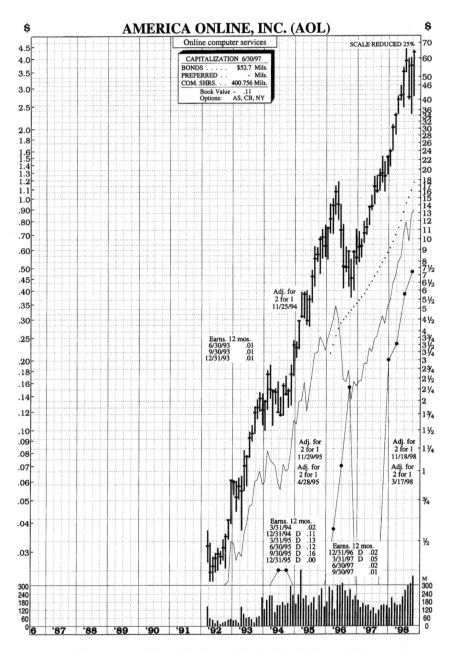

Online computer services

SCALE REDUCED 25%

CAPITALIZATION 6/30/97	
BONDS	$52.7 Mils.
PREFERRED . .	- Mils.
COM. SHRS. . .	400.756 Mils.
Book Value - .11	
Options: AS, CB, NY	

Adj. for
2 for 1
11/25/94

Earns. 12 mos.
6/30/93   .01
9/30/93   .01
12/31/93   .01

Adj. for
2 for 1
11/29/95

Adj. for
2 for 1
4/28/95

Adj. for
2 for 1
11/18/98

Adj. for
2 for 1
3/17/98

Earns. 12 mos.
3/31/94   .02
12/31/94 D .11
3/31/95   D .13
6/30/95   D .12
9/30/95   D .16
12/31/95 D .00

Earns. 12 mos.
12/31/96 D .02
3/31/97   D .05
6/30/97   .02
9/30/97   .01

'87 '88 '89 '90 '91 '92 '93 '94 '95 '96 '97 '98

Chart courtesy of Securities Research Co. Reprinted with permission.

years of investing in a customer base would prove fruitful. It wasn't that simple, of course. The company faced constant accusations that it overstated both its subscriber base and the length of time that subscribers stayed with the source. Only after a horrendous year in 1996 (and a major accounting restatement that went with it) did those catcalls dissipate. When AOL raised its subscriber fees by $2 per month early in 1998, the visionaries could take a moment to grin. *Fortune* magazine ran Steve Case on the cover with the headline "And the Winner is . . . AOL." The stock proceeded to double yet again. Whether or not you participated in the 1998 surge, it is a perfect example of why the "acceptance" phenomenon outlined in the introduction is so destructive when it comes to visionary investments. The specific form of acceptance I'm referring to is when investors permanently shun a stock just because they missed a particularly good purchase point. Lost in this self-flagellation is the fact that a well-positioned company can get even better, which somehow is less intuitive than the notion that a down-and-out company can stage a comeback. But either situation can make you money: To prove the point, AOL shares doubled *yet again* while this manuscript was being proofread!

PITFALLS

The most obvious pitfall that a visionary can experience is being wrong. Solar energy did not make oil heat obsolete. The Wankel engine did not supplant conventional automotive technology. The Home Shopping Network did not devour the entire retailing world. When you're wrong, you can be really, really wrong, and the world is terribly unfair in its judgment. If you have the audacity to head an enterprise whose vision doesn't come to pass, you spend the rest of your life being compared to John DeLorean.

However, as a stockholder and not a company founder, you shouldn't have the problem of having all your eggs in one basket. Diversification is a must. Besides, being wrong is only one of many problems encountered by a visionary. Believe it or not, although I've touted America Online as a visionary's stock, AOL also demonstrates a classic trap for the visionary, which is prematurely calling an end to an era.

Recall that much of the wall of worry that AOL stock climbed was based on investors' fears that the heyday of the online service would be short-lived and that providers of cheap, direct Internet access would eventually win out. In other words, there were self-proclaimed visionaries who concluded that AOL's good times would be too fleeting to warrant investment.

I was reminded of the similar shroud that investors placed over Blockbuster Video, whose cash-cow video rental business was seen by many to be doomed by the emergence of pay-per-view. A few years before that, another group of quasi-visionaries saw Federal Express's breakout success as the inevitable victim of changing technologies. But be aware that the "inevitable" can take a long, long time. Even though technological advances can create the threat of obsolescence in a wide variety of businesses, *true franchises are much harder to destroy*. Blockbuster, FedEx, and AOL all created true franchises, and visions of their early demise could only be made through Coke-bottle glasses.

A related factor that visionary investors have to contend with is that their investments tend to be controversial, and holding the stock can require an ability to deal with a sea of negativism. Remember, when you're in the middle of the action, you don't know for certain that the story is going to turn out well. At a minimum, you have to be comfortable with the company's accounting methods and with its future equity needs. The last thing you need is for the company to lack the capital to make good on its dreams. If undercapitalization leads to future equity offerings, those offerings can be dilutive to existing shareholders, whose long-term vision overlooked the company's intermediate-term requirements.

GAME PLAN

If you, like me, find yourself a bit depressed upon reading about *other* people's visions, take heart. Even if you never have a powerful vision in your life, you can make money just the same.

Do you remember the children's story *The Big Jump?* The story centered around a young boy's need to make a seemingly impossible leap from one object to another one far out in the distance. The task was eventually solved the old-fashioned way—by going one step at a time. Upon hearing this ending as a six-year-old, I found the solution a bit of a letdown. At age six I had yet to learn that life doesn't have that many magical moments; most of our victories are hard-earned, and they take time. Even the biggest visionaries have to hold onto their stocks one day at a time, and so can you. An architect might have more vision than a mason, but both can participate in the creation of a special building.

You know what? Not everyone can predict their success stories, even if they're right on top of the situation. Consider Compaq Computer, whose 1998 merger with Digital Equipment created a computing giant that trailed only IBM in annual revenues. Who could have predicted such an outcome back in 1982 when Digital was the world leader in minicomputers and Compaq was created to make clones of IBM PCs? "In the early eighties, if we had thought of one day displacing IBM in PCs and rivaling it in size overall, we would have made good candidates for the loony bin," said Compaq chairman Ben Rosen to *Time* magazine. Moral: If a company's management is surprised at the extent of their success, don't be ashamed to admit your own surprise.

One of the major fallacies of hypergrowth investing is that you need to see the whole success story coming in order to invest. All too often, visionary-type stocks create a polarization between the believers and the nonbelievers, who become table-pounding investors and cynics, respectively. But it is perfectly reasonable to invest a smaller amount in a company whose ideas "just might work," knowing that the payoff for success can be extraordinary. The more confidence you feel, the more you should be willing to put down.

I am reminded of the old TV game show *I'll Bet,* on which contestants bet whether their spouses could answer specific questions. Contestants had choices for the size of their wagers: $100, $50, $25, or even nothing. Incredibly, many participants would say, "I'll bet $100," and *then* they'd pause to think about whether their spouse could answer the question. How about betting in proportion to your confidence level, rather than opting for the maximum while you're still uncomfortable? That was the whole purpose of the choices!

If you can feel the investment analogue coming, perhaps I've given away too much, but here goes. When it comes to high-growth stocks, you don't have to invest a huge sum at your first possible opportunity. You can put a little bit down and then adjust, knowing that if the company does end up prospering, even your modest initial investment will prove very worthwhile. That's pretty much the strategy the best growth fund managers follow with every passing day.

 # Personality Spotlight

The Control Freak

In discussing the visionary, one point that lay under the surface was the tremendous advantage the shareholder has over the people who actually run the company. Unlike Fred Smith of FedEx, Jerry Yang of Yahoo!, or any of the other leaders who slaved to see their visions become reality, a shareholder barely has to do anything. It's an incredible deal, when you think about it.

Aha, but there is one very big psychological distinction between the positions of shareholder and CEO, which is one of *control.* When times go bad, as they did for FedEx, AOL, and any other growing company you could think of, people within the company can at least do something about it. The poor shareholder can no more make things better than an airline passenger can eliminate clear-air turbulence. It's no wonder that the mood at investment institutions is often far less self-assured than the mood at the company itself. It's also no wonder that control freak investors are among the first to bail out in times of crisis.

If lack of control is an issue for you, then you may need to take some nonstandard steps to make the stock market a more comfortable place for you. Shareholder activism is one way: Attend the annual meeting. Ask questions. Make sure you vote for whom you want to see on the board of directors. In short, do everything you can to make yourself feel like part of the active management process.

Believe it or not, many people who are afraid of flying become much more relaxed in a small plane when they are seated right next to the pilot. The secret is that a layer of distrust has been removed. The pilot, it turns out, is a human being; the tilting of the plane is deliberate and in the pilot's control, and you can see it. By forming mental images of this comfortable setting, even the bigger planes become a lot easier to deal with.

Investors with control issues are involved in a similar battle of mind over matter. To win this battle, you want your image of the company to be what you saw on your last visit, not what you're looking at on your office Quotron. The former is both exciting and reassuring, whereas the latter can be discomfiting. Once you overcome that discomfort, you're in a better position to hold your growth stocks for the long term.

"Now _there's_ a complicated wolf."

THE
CONTRARIAN

To many folks, contrarianism is what investing in the stock market is all about. There's nothing better than buying at times when everybody else is scared, unless it's selling when shares are the most popular. That's the idea, anyway. A contrarian lives to be different.

Contrarianism is in some sense easier to identify than our other personality categories, as there are hundreds of questions I could have used in the little personality quiz. Many of us have witnessed contrarian behavior from a very early age, as in those kids who chose burnt sienna as their favorite Crayola color: Did they actually like brown, or did they just like being different? A generation later, those same kids might have discovered that the stock market provides plenty of opportunities to put their world view to work.

ARE YOU A CONTRARIAN?

Answer these questions and find out:

1 Did you really think that the Dave Clark Five was going to edge out The Beatles?

> *You may not have realized it at the time, but your preference for the underdog might have been instinctive, rather than being based on an assessment of the music.*

2 If you're placing a drive-thru order at McDonald's and you are told to pay at the first window, do you wonder whether they mean the one in front (the first window from the street) or the one in the back (the first window you come across)?

> *Overthinking is a classic contrarian trap.*

3 If a fender-bender occurs at a dangerous intersection and the mayor then pontificates about the need to make the town's streets safer, do you find yourself wondering why in the world the problem wasn't corrected earlier?

> *Contrarians derive much more satisfaction from their actions when those actions are anticipatory in character.*

4 When you scored big on IBM's turnaround beginning in 1994, did it annoy you that so many other investors shared your gains?

> *Contrarians rarely like company. Companies, yes. Company, no.*

5 Were you the second, the third, or even the fourth child in your family?

> *In the words of Jared Diamond, as quoted by Stephen Jay Gould, "Since firstborns already occupy their own niches, laterborns, if they are to be noticed, have to find unoccupied niches."*

BRIGHT SPOTS

The most visible and possibly the most fruitful application of contrarianism is buying shares of companies that are wrongly considered to be on their last legs. The classic example would be Chrysler in the early 1980s, before the Federal bailout, the minivan, and the overall Iacocca magic. By 1987, when the Federal monies were paid back in full and ahead of schedule, Chrysler shares had appreciated over 2500 percent from their 1981 low. Somewhere along the way, with a tidy profit in hand, a contrarian could have contentedly sold, on the grounds that the hoped-for recovery had in fact taken place.

You don't even have to wander that far back into market history to find great contrary plays. USAir was a $4 stock in 1995. Two USAir planes had gone down in the prior year. The company was in technical violation of its debt covenants. Warren Buffett had written down his controversial position in USAir preferred stock by 75 percent. The entire airline industry was reeling, and survival could not be assured. So what happened? Within a few short years, the Dow Jones Transportation Average ended up hitting new highs, a reflection of the airline industry's return to prosperity. And as the industry's most embattled participant, USAir was also the biggest beneficiary of the upswing. By 1998, it was trading at over *$70* per share.

To many if not most investors, these stocks would have seemed absurdly risky. And just because this particular pair worked out stupendously doesn't mean there were no risks involved. Only later can we say that they were *wrongly* considered to be on their last legs; and for every glistening success story of their kind, there are perhaps five or six stories that clutter the bankruptcy rolls. The playing field of a contrarian is fraught with peril, filled with companies that you really can't invest in without a disproportionate share of legwork.

Of course, the extraordinary rewards of this type of investing can make an entire portfolio a winner even if there are pockmarks along the way. This approach is familiar to venture capitalists, many of whom seem to laugh off their failures on the way to Fort Knox. But the point is that the contrarian has a real advantage in finding these stocks because any sense of danger is dwarfed by the excitement of a truly different idea that *no one* else would be investing in.

A Different Form of Visions and Bargains

Turnaround stocks such as Chrysler and USAir were of course *losing* money at their ideal purchase points. As a practical matter, investing in situations like these requires every bit as much foresight as our friend the visionary, but note that the visionary is typically more interested in growth companies than in turnaround stories.

When it comes to finding contrarian ideas from profitable companies, it almost goes without saying that the place to start is among companies whose price/earnings ratios (P/Es) are well below that of the overall market. This approach should be familiar to readers of *Forbes,* where investment counselor David Dreman—author of *The New Contrarian Investment Strategy*—has had a regular column for many years.

We talked about low P/E stocks at length in the bargain hunter chapter, but many of them just aren't sexy enough for the real contrarian. One class of stocks that contrarians might find to their liking would be mislabeled fad stocks. A great prototype for this category is Reebok in 1985. The company had just come public and the stock was flying; but the accepted word on the Street was that aerobic shoes were just a fad, suggesting that the stock was destined to come back to earth. The fad perception was so automatic that few bothered to notice that Reebok actually had a *low* P/E. This apparent contradiction was reconciled by Robert Malloy of Merrill Lynch (the firm that brought Reebok public), who exclaimed, "The only thing going up faster than Reebok stock is the earnings estimate." Reebok shares rose 400 percent in their first year.

First Team Sports, makers of Ultra-Wheels inline skates, performed a similar high-wire act a few years later, riding the unexpected longevity of the rollerblade craze to a 15-fold gain. Again, the investors who profited were those willing to go against the accepted wisdom that rollerblading was merely a fad. Score another point for the contrarians.

PITFALLS

So far our contrarianism has led us to some wonderful out-of-the-way winners. But you may have noticed that these ideas don't exactly arise every day. In between these high points, it might come as no surprise that contrarians are routinely tripped up by their overwhelming desire to be different.

The underlying issue is that originality isn't always a prescription for success because investing is much different than, say, competitive athletics. When Pete Sampras gives a clinic on how to serve, he doesn't really expect that anyone in the class is going to do it as well as he can. But you or I could literally match Warren Buffett's stock market performance. If he owns shares of American Express, so can I; if he owns Gillette, I can, too. Any one of us could duplicate his entire portfolio if we wanted to.

However, not everyone is content being a copycat, and contrarians take this aversion to an extreme. As a contrarian, you are so determined to be different that year after year goes by and you never, ever call your broker to buy American Express, even though you know in your heart and in your spreadsheet that it is a superior company. Your contrarian streak won't let you make that phone call. Your internal voice cries out, "That's Buffett's stock," and so it remains. *Contrarians cannot bring themselves to buy stocks of popular companies, no matter how strong the investment case may be.*

Merck. Johnson & Johnson. Disney. Coca-Cola. Microsoft. Fannie Mae. McDonald's. Compaq. Intel. Look closely at this list. Do you see a single company that a card-carrying contrarian would have anything to do with? Yet anyone with a pulse knows how much money you could have made on any of these great companies over the past 5, 10, 15 years, or whatever. Perhaps the enduring legacy of the great bull market is that you don't need to be original to succeed. Is it any wonder that you don't hear as much about contrarianism as you used to?

Selling Too Soon

If you're a dyed-in-the-wool contrarian, you might have an automatic reaction upon seeing a chart such as the one on page 63. The knee-jerk reaction is that the good times can't possibly continue forever. The stock appears to have gotten ahead of itself at least temporarily, and possibly permanently. That's how the picture would look to contrarians, anyway, many of whom make their money by latching on to a stock early and getting out early, lest they be caught holding a popular stock after all.

But once you get the knee-jerk response out of the way, you should take the time to notice that the company with this marvelously upbeat chart has yet to be identified. I won't hold you in suspense. The stock in question is Dell Computer. The reason for the decline in the middle was that the company had an unfortunate experience with derivative securities, an experience that obliterated a full year's worth of earnings and shook investor confidence for months afterward. The derivative fallout was the type of buying opportunity that contrarians covet and do so well at: a solid, growing company whose earnings and share price happen to get derailed by a nonrecurring event. You buy when the very mention of the name sends shudders through your competition at the trust funds, and you sell when the company is back on track. In that fashion, you could have quintupled your money on Dell between 1993 and 1995.

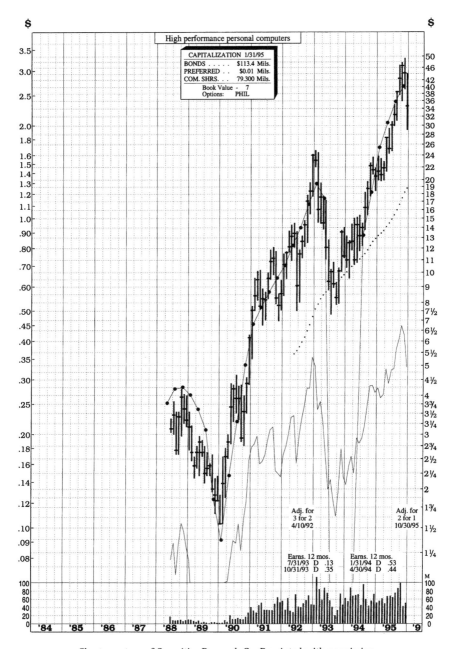

Chart courtesy of Securities Research Co. Reprinted with permission.

Now for the bad news, at least for the sell-too-soon branch of the contrarian party. Here's how Dell performed in the two years following the preceding chart. (See chart on page 65.)

I don't really think I have to add too much, except to say that knee-jerk judgments should never be an investor's guiding force. Whereas visionaries sometimes sell too soon because they foresee a specific future problem, contrarians often sell on principle, forgetting that being back on track can be merely a prelude to outstanding future growth. Yes, Dell Computer was an exceptional company with an exceptional chart, but that's the whole point. It's hard enough to find such a stock in the first place. If you were right there and bailed prematurely, the psychic cost can be considerable.

False Hopes

As we just saw, contrarians are among the first to give up on an emerging winner once the company reaches a certain level of popularity. This attitude not only leads to selling too soon, it can also lead to situations where a proven leader is rejected in favor of a mere upstart. A typical contrarian reaction is, "I may have missed that particular software/fast food/semiconductor/waste disposal stock, but I'm ready for the next great software/fast food/semiconductor/waste disposal stock that comes along." Remember, buying at anything but the absolute bottom is anathema to contrarians. Therefore, in the vernacular of this book's introduction, these investors are especially early to "accept" the fact that they missed out.

To see what a prescription for disaster this form of acceptance can be, imagine that you're a single businessman about to embark on a three-hour bus ride. To your surprise and delight, you look up to see a ravishing brunette just about to reach your row. (If the political incorrectness of the setting troubles you, then also imagine that the story takes place in 1954.) Alas, your briefcase and assorted papers have taken up the seat beside you, so you watch helplessly as the femme fatale

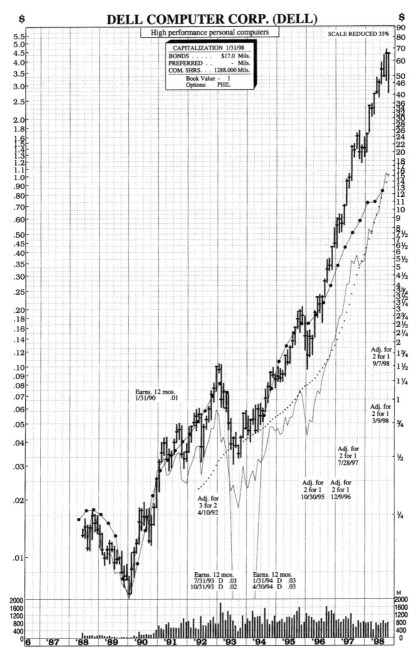

DELL COMPUTER CORP. (DELL)

High performance personal computers

SCALE REDUCED 35%

CAPITALIZATION 1/31/98
BONDS . . . . . $17.0 Mils.
PREFERRED . .   - Mils.
COM. SHRS. . . . 1288.000 Mils.
Book Value -   1
Options: PHIL

Earns. 12 mos.
1/31/90   .01

Adj. for
2 for 1
9/7/98

Adj. for
2 for 1
3/9/98

Adj. for
2 for 1
7/28/97

Adj. for   Adj. for
2 for 1   2 for 1
10/30/95   12/9/96

Adj. for
3 for 2
4/10/92

Earns. 12 mos.   Earns. 12 mos.
7/31/93 D .01   1/31/94 D .03
10/31/93 D .02   4/30/94 D .03

Chart courtesy of Securities Research Co. Reprinted with permission.

glides by toward the back. What do you do? Naturally, you grab your briefcase and papers and place them on your lap. This reaction is instinctive and seems to make perfect sense. After all, now that you know the possibilities, you're ready for the next gorgeous creature who comes along. But have you forgotten that you're on a *bus?*

What contrarians overlook is that their instinctive preference for the next great company within a given industry is really a veiled insult to the one-of-a-kind qualities possessed by the leader. The result of this stance is often a woeful triple whammy, wherein it turns out that (1) the second wave of companies never comes close to challenging the leader, (2) the one that got away hadn't really gotten away at all because there was plenty of growth remaining for the leader, and (3) worst having come to worst, the leader's subsequent advances are specifically at the expense of the also-rans.

This triple whammy can be put to work. In 1993, when I had to come up with 10 "stocks to avoid" each month for *Worth* magazine, I concluded that it wasn't too late to include software stocks such as Borland International and Novell, even though the companies' fundamentals were already in decline and even though the stocks had already come down a lot. I could just hear subscribers cackling "*Now* he tells us to sell. Where was he two years ago?" Well, point granted, but basic psychology suggested that the share prices were still inflated by contrarians looking for the next Microsoft. In the five years that followed, the fundamentals of both companies remained poor, and one by one, the contrarians gave up. Borland and Novell each fell an additional 50 percent or even more during one of the greatest winning streaks in stock market history.

Too Right

If all this weren't bad enough, the final dreadful predicament that contrarians lapse into is that when they are right, they can be too right for their own good. What use is it, after all, to be ahead of the curve when you can never make money until other investors agree with your contrary idea? The "better" your idea, the longer you may have to wait.

You could have glommed on to Chrysler in 1979, only to face a two-year wait and a 66 percent loss before the real turnaround began. You could have bought USAir at $20 per share in 1993 and been forced to suffer as it plummeted to just $4 in the next 18 months. Staying on for the happy ending was no mean feat. Warren Buffett couldn't bear to hold on to his USAir preferred stock the whole way through.* Why should you? The act of waiting, being characterized by the lack of both productivity and control, is one of the most stressful things we humans can undergo.

Sir John Templeton, perhaps the dean of all contrary investors, has endured more than his share of hopeful waiting. For example, he invested heavily in European stocks on the heels of the Marshall Plan and was rewarded when other investors finally noticed the post–World War II economic boom. But as his career wore on, Templeton tired of the waiting process. In *The Money Masters,* author John Train noted, "If one of two otherwise similar stocks is just starting to attract interest and the other is still in eclipse, then [Templeton] gives preference to the one that is starting to move." There is a key distinction here. Long-term investing certainly implies a *willingness* to wait, but no one said a long wait was mandatory.

Contrarians are notably reluctant to shift gears in the way that Templeton did, so we can admire him for having taken action. But we can also hope that any shifting you may have to do comes more swiftly.

---

* Buffett tried on more than one occasion to unload his shares. As luck would have it, the complicated nature of his ownership position caused those attempts to fall through, so he participated in the dramatic recovery rather than selling at 50 percent of face value. He summarized his USAir acumen in the 1996 Berkshire Hathaway annual report, in which he quoted a friend as asking him, "If you're so rich, why aren't you smart?"

GAME PLAN

If you've been victimized by your contrariness in the market, chances are you need to enlarge the playing field. In other words, you may have to find a graceful way to buy some of those stocks you've been sticking your nose up at all these years.

When it comes to your aversion to popular, well-established companies—the kind that you shunned permanently on hearing John Templeton say, "It takes no skill or training to buy"—there is another approach. Remember, what turns you on is being different, and you still have a chance to be different if you resolve to know more about these companies than anyone else. What was Pfizer's average return on equity even *before* Viagra was introduced? A healthy 28 percent, natch. What was the 100th country to have a McDonald's outlet? Belarus, of course. You may not be the only one making money on these stocks, but you should have no trouble convincing yourself that the others don't deserve their gains as much as you do.

The key to this approach is to admit that the whole contrary strategy is laden with ego. No, I'm not being critical. Freud had no problem giving everyone an ego, and far be it from me to disagree with Freud. If you had to hire a money manager, would you rather have one with a big ego or no ego? Just as I thought. So let's be honest, all you contrarians out there. The reason you've been unwilling to go along with your fellow citizens isn't because you feel unworthy of *them*, is it?

If that approach doesn't suit, there's another, quite different way to enlarge your playing field. Leo Dworsky, a good friend of mine and one-time manager of the Fidelity Contrafund, makes the insightful point that contrarian investing, far from its popular perception, needn't apply only to those companies that are down and almost out. Nor does it restrict itself to companies with low P/Es. As we saw in the Visionary chapter, wasn't "everyone" (some visionaries included) saying that America Online was going to bust? For that very reason, you could have made the case that AOL, however seemingly extraordinary its price, was actually a contrarian investment. And as fate would have it, its extraordinarily high price became even more extraordinary in the years that followed. (As if on cue, Will Danoff, one of Dworsky's successors at the Contrafund helm, owned about as much AOL as he could—though he'd be the first to admit that filling a $30 billion fund entirely with contrary ideas takes some linguistic tinkering. But he did it, and so can you.)

Ultimately, a contrarian's game plan is to notice where your short-falls lie and to take corrective action. If you consistently sell too soon, try holding on longer. If you never seem to make money on an industry leader, well, bring yourself to buy the next leader you can. These types of corrective action can make sense for any category of investor, but remember that you as a contrarian have a tremendous advantage in their implementation. After all, what I'm really asking you to do is not so much to change your pattern, but to consider—every once in a while, that is—being contrary to yourself.

 Personality Spotlight

Stubbornness

You may have noticed that you can't be a real contrarian without being a tad on the stubborn side. The reason this observation is important is that stubbornness isn't always thought of as being a positive personality characteristic, but it can be a great help in your pursuit of investment success.

For a good example of this quality at work, I go back to a conversation I had with Jay Nelson, a long-time media and consumer products analyst with Brown Brothers Harriman. Nelson was relating his experience with

Tele-Communications, Inc. (TCI), the nation's second-largest cable television company. He had recommended the stock at just north of $20 per share in 1995, and he had to contend with any number of anxious clients as it sank to $11, amid concern that TCI chairman John Malone was not extracting value from the company's considerable asset base.

The story had a very happy ending. The first part of the TCI recovery took place in 1997, when the stock rebounded into the mid-20s amid a more favorable outlook for the pricing of cable services. Then, in the summer of 1998, AT&T announced that it would purchase Tele-Communications for $50 per share.

Well, I checked back with Jay Nelson, and he admitted that there was a major dose of stubbornness in his decision to stick with the stock, above and beyond his analytical determination that it didn't belong at $11 per share. He also had the humility to point out that even after the buyout offer, the stock had "only" doubled since his first recommendation, meaning that it really hadn't outperformed the market by much. But to view his experience with the stock in that light would be shortsighted. We'd all love to win in straight sets if we could, but there is a special irreplaceable psychic factor to a comeback. Besides, those whose conviction translates into additional purchases during the downward phase will come out way, way ahead. (In TCI's case, the stock spurted to $70 in early 1999!)

I think that many of us can point to at least one stock with which we had a similar experience. Looking back, I have to say that my biggest disappointments in the stock market are not the times I've been wrong, but the occasions in which I haven't have the conviction to ride out a great investment that had the nerve to start out poorly. Similarly, the most satisfying victories, even if not the numerically most valuable, were in recommendations like CompUSA, where the early going was treacherous but the end results made it all worthwhile.

Whether Tele-Communications and CompUSA were victories for stubbornness becomes a matter of splitting hairs. In our society, we typically reserve our judgments of stubbornness for those decisions that have gone wrong; when things turn out well instead, we get a better-sounding adjective, something like *perseverance* or *steadfastness.* Whatever we call it, remember that the main reason a contrarian buys a stock is because the market is wrong. Therefore, there is no point in being a contrarian unless you are stubborn enough to maintain that view, whatever the short-term cost, until the market finally comes to its senses and agrees with you.

"Emily, a Mr. Barnes and a Mr. Noble would like a word with you."

THE
SENTIMENTALIST

The sentimentalist is at the opposite pole from our friend the visionary. A visionary sees things the way they never were and asks, "Why not?" The sentimentalist sees things the way they are and says, "Looks good to me." In the sentimentalist's vocabulary, *change* is a four-letter word.

Of all of the personality types we will be considering, the sentimentalist is semantically the least blessed. Whereas a visionary or a contrarian sounds like a great investor even before we get to the fine points, a sentimentalist sounds like a babe in the woods. However, rest assured that this personality type has strengths and weaknesses just like any other. Besides, most of us are members of the sentimentalist club, and I'm certainly no exception. An aversion to change is as inherently human as an aversion to snakes.

The one concession I will make is to reverse our usual order of business. Because the investment hurdles a sentimentalist faces are so fundamental, I wanted to get them out of the way before getting to the good stuff.

ARE YOU A SENTIMENTALIST?

Answer these questions and find out:

1 Would you lobby hard to prevent Wal-Mart from entering your community?

> *That is, if you happen to live in the three or four communities in the United States that Wal-Mart hasn't entered already.*

2 When you go to a restaurant or bar you haven't been to in five years, are you disappointed when you find that the songs on the jukebox have changed?

> *"Come Go with Me" by the Del-Vikings was on the first jukebox I ever saw, sometime in the late 1950s. Nobody told me it wasn't going to be there forever, and it took until 1970 or so before I finally figured that out.*

3 As you hold the stock of a company that is steadily losing market share, do you pride yourself on being a long-term investor?

> *Spin doctoring, sentimentalist-style. When long-term obsolescence is in store, short-term investing just might be the best way to go.*

4 Are you troubled with the idea of investing in companies that constantly have to reinvent themselves to stay ahead?

> *Many companies don't have to, so maybe you can be a sentimentalist and win out after all.*

5 Are you a first-born?

> *Again, to quote Stephen Jay Gould, "[Firstborns] tend to grow up competent and confident, but also conservative and unlikely to favor quirkiness or innovation. Why threaten an existing structure that has always offered you clear advantages over siblings?"*

PITFALLS

On the buy side, sentimentalists encounter difficulties because they just can't bring themselves to own certain groups of stocks that might be good for their financial health. In this sense the sentimentalist is a distant cousin of the ethical investor. As you may know, ethical investors (I do so hate this term, what with its nasty implications for the rest of us) automatically swear off such fields as tobacco, alcohol, and anything else that might be deemed impure. The ethical folks can on occasion get tiresome with their preachiness, but they deserve some credit. Many have done extremely well over the years, either by first-rate stock selection within their restricted investment universes or by taking advantage of the fact that these universes have been stuffed with the simon-pure Intels of the world and not the sludge-ridden Union Carbides.

Sentimentalists aren't quite as lucky. At their core, they are ethical investors whose inner voice has told them that anything new is unethical!

To see how unhelpful this emotional backdrop can be, you need look no further than retail stocks. Consider that the single most dominant theme in retail investing over the past 20 years has been the advantage of economies of scale. Larger chains, by buying in bulk, can obtain their merchandise at prices that simply aren't available to the proverbial corner drugstore. The neighborhood stationery store is similarly disadvantaged, not being able to cope with the likes of Staples, Office Depot, or whatever giant happens to lurk in the area. But the sentimentalists aren't the ones investing in these companies or any other purveyors of change. If anything, they're the people trying to make sure that Wal-Mart, McDonald's, and all other personifications of evil never break into their neighborhoods.

What sentimentalists have to realize is that their choices, like any ethical choices, are highly personal matters. If you don't want to invest in tobacco companies because you associate their product with the killing of America's youth, that's fine; you'll have plenty of company. But if you don't want to invest in Hewlett-Packard or Texas Instruments—they're the ones making the calculators that kill off those same youth, one brain cell at a time—at least be aware that your preferences may not match those of the general populace.

Sentimentalists specialize in *generational* preferences, which can be especially tricky to jettison because generational phenomena often seem eternal to the beholder. As a baby boomer, I grew up thinking that automobiles were huge chrome structures with fins, because that's what I saw in people's driveways until the 1950s had the nerve to end. More generally, widespread nostalgia for the days of the nuclear family obscures the fact that the Ozzie-and-Harriet era was merely one fleeting stage in America's evolution, not an absolute standard. If you can't recognize the difference between what is generational and what is enduring, the stock market will be happy to alert you. But by then it can be too late.

Book retailing provides investors with a great example of how important it can be to switch gears. If you missed the first transition, in which local booksellers were displaced by the likes of B. Dalton and Waldenbooks, you didn't miss much because the two weren't standalone public companies. However, dominance soon shifted to Barnes & Noble and Borders, whose superstores blew away the medium-sized chains (and which ended up owning B. Dalton and Waldenbooks, respectively). Barnes & Noble shares advanced 200 percent in the five years following its 1993 IPO. Borders did even better, quadrupling in its first three years. But if you somehow managed to get sentimental over these two companies, you might have missed the latest generation of book retailers. Shares of Amazon.com gained 600 percent within a year of the company's 1997 IPO, and that was only the beginning.

When it comes to the sell side of the investment equation, sentimentalists consistently get into trouble by violating the age-old maxim, "Don't fall in love with a stock." This maxim originates from the peril of getting attached to a company or a product and being unwilling to see how change is leaving it behind. We've already mentioned Macintosh users, whose sentimentality didn't prevent Apple Computer from experiencing a decade-long slump. The rise and fall of Wang Labs in the early 1980s was even more precipitous. Investors would have done well to recognize that the company's success was not generic ("Wang is a great company") but instead rested on a very specific product—the dedicated word processing station—that was destined to become technologically obsolete. Talk about a love affair gone sour. As Louis Rukeyser wrote in 1976 in *How to Make Money in Wall Street,* "The only love an investor should ever seek is love for sale."

BRIGHT SPOTS

There is, however, at least one ray of hope. Fast forward to May of 1997, when I was conducting a routine interview with Ely Callaway, the eponymous leader of the fabulously successful Callaway Golf company. Apparently he had never read Rukeyser's book, because he stoutly maintained that "you simply have to fall in love with a company." That's what he did, of course, and there's no denying his record. As we saw in the introduction, Callaway Golf has endured plenty of turbulence since its IPO in 1992, but that didn't stop the stock from going up almost 1000 percent in its first five years.

Whom are we to believe? It's purely a matter of interpretation. If by *love* you mean a purely blind devotion, as in "a face only a mother could love," the investment negatives are clear. However, if love means "passion," everything changes. Callaway's point is that unless you have a powerful emotional attachment to a company, you'll never make it through the bad times. In this way, Ely Callaway the visionary seems oddly sympatico with Ely Callaway the sentimentalist. The link is that a visionary's long road to success is inevitably plagued by the sort of lumps that only a devoted investor can deal with.

Even those of us who have yet to place their first buy order can recognize the type of attachment to which Callaway is referring because it exists in all facets of our lives, notably within family life. Can you imagine how splintered society would be if we all shed our parents or siblings whenever we became uncomfortable with them? Without being too, er, sentimental, it's fair to say that our efforts to repair relationships, whether familial, marital, or just between friends, almost always leave us with something more than what we started with. In the case of marriage, it's not uncommon to want to bag the whole thing; but our chosen contract doesn't let us out quite that easily, and I have yet to find anyone, happily married or happily divorced, who really thinks that an easier exit hatch would have been a better way to go.

Sorry for the digression. I guess I'm just tired of seeing passion get such a bad rap on Wall Street when it is plainly the foundation for every business success that we investors try so desperately to find.

A different type of bright spot for the sentimentalist is that there are companies that have *benefited* by creating a limited but timeless product profile. For example, when you invest in Mattel, you are basically making an investment in the staying power of the Barbie franchise. Barbie was introduced in 1959, and forty years later accounted for 40 percent of Mattel's sales, with more than two dolls sold each second worldwide. Johnson & Johnson carries a huge product inventory, but its single most profitable product is none other than the Band-Aid, introduced in the 1920s. And although it's more difficult psychologically to cozy up to the IRS, H&R Block is a company whose basic business is literally as inviolable as life, death, and taxes.

The foregoing praise should not be construed as a permanent stock recommendation because all companies face challenges. Mattel took out some Barbie insurance by purchasing the American Girl line in 1998 perhaps presaging the earnings shortfall announced later that year. H&R Block investors constantly fret about the specter of a revamped U.S. tax code. But all of these companies have reliable cash flows derived from proven businesses, and the brand recognition of these businesses makes it all but impossible for a competitor to displace them. I know of several first-rate investors who deal *exclusively* with stocks such as these, not for sentimental reasons, but because future earnings can be predicted with unusual accuracy.

When Sentimentalists Go Too Far

So there is good to offset the bad for the sentimentalist, as we had hoped. And as with all our investment personalities, the challenge for sentimental investors is to determine when they've gone too far. The easy answer is to say that they've gone too far when an investment becomes untouchable.

To see what untouchability looks like, the best example from my personal experience came in 1986, when I was working at a small investment firm whose clients were almost all individuals (as opposed to institutions such as endowments and pension plans). One client was a family whose name I've long since forgotten, but whose main holding—Borden—remains etched in my memory. At the time, the entire brand-name packaged-food sector was experiencing a tremendous boom. The economy was continuing to recover from the early eighties' recession, and these companies found that they held considerable pricing power, as in "if a bowl of cereal costs five cents more, no one will care." But that extra nickel was pure profit, which led to some tremendous earnings and stock price advances for the entire sector, Borden included.

The result of this boom was that Borden became an absolute untouchable in this client's portfolio, which in turn created a powerful disincentive for me ever to have an opinion on the stock. As the chief analyst (it was a small firm), I'd be in a strictly lose-lose position if I ever recommended selling the stock. If I was wrong, I'd never hear the end of it. And if I was right, I'd still lose out, for I would be the messenger with the news that no one wanted to hear.

As it happened, Borden scratched out a few more decent years, but when the 1990s arrived, the company became the absolute worst performer of the packaged-food sector (see chart on page 81). In sharp contrast to its peer group, Borden steadfastly refused to spend any money on advertising, and the result was a dramatic drop in brand recognition for corporate mascot Elsie the Cow. By the time of this decline I was working at Fidelity, having become a writer first and an analyst second. But I often wondered whether that particular family held its Borden shares until the bitter end, because that's what sentimentalists usually do. The company was eventually forced to sell out in 1994, by which time the share price had dropped 70 percent from its 1989 high.

Ah, but *why* does an investment become untouchable? This is a fascinating subject that sentimentalists would do well to explore. Clinically speaking, a reluctance to sell is associated with a retentive personality. Retentive personalities view their possessions (stocks included) as extensions of themselves, and in that light selling becomes roughly equivalent to cutting off an arm or a leg. Here's the crucial issue: Rather than own up to this personality pattern, the retentive/sentimentalist will invariably create defenses that enable the pattern to continue. Defenses as in lame excuses not to sell.

The precise nature of the defense depends on whether the stock in question is near its peak or has already fallen off. In the case of stocks that are showing a healthy profit, sentimental investors have an unlikely accomplice in the form of the Internal Revenue Service. "I can't possibly sell. It'll cost a fortune in capital gains taxes!" Nonsense. However perverse you may think the U.S. tax code is, it isn't designed to reward you for clinging to a stock that's past its prime. Selling doesn't actually cost you money. The reason people feel otherwise is that the value of a stock holding on the monthly appraisal or brokerage statement does not reflect taxes (of course) because the precise tax implications of a particular sale will vary greatly between different individuals. So if you see $20,000 worth of Borden on your statement, why should you sell and see your net proceeds chopped to $16,000 or whatever? Unfortunately, if there's no better reason to hold on, you shouldn't be

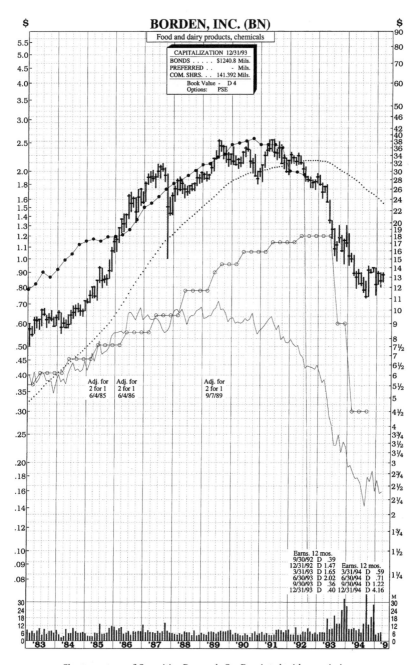

BORDEN, INC. (BN)

Food and dairy products, chemicals

CAPITALIZATION 12/31/93
BONDS . . . . . $1240.8 Mils.
PREFERRED . .   - Mils.
COM. SHRS. . . .   141.392 Mils.
Book Value -   D 4
Options: PSE

Adj. for
2 for 1
6/4/85

Adj. for
2 for 1
6/4/86

Adj. for
2 for 1
9/7/89

Earns. 12 mos.
9/30/92 D .39
12/31/92 D 1.47   Earns. 12 mos.
3/31/93 D 1.65   3/31/94 D .59
6/30/93 D 2.02   6/30/94 D .71
9/30/93 D .36   9/30/94 D 1.22
12/31/93 D .40   12/31/94 D 4.16

'83 '84 '85 '86 '87 '88 '89 '90 '91 '92 '93 '94 '9

Chart courtesy of Securities Research Co. Reprinted with permission.

surprised to see the stock's pre-tax value drop below $16,000 and keep on dropping.

Which brings us to the second case. If the stock in question has already fallen from its highs, sentimentalists find a different reason to hold on. I call it the dollar-lined fallacy because more times than we'd care to admit, what we're sentimental about is the price at which the stock used to be trading, and nothing more. The warm and fuzzy feeling? Forget it. It's cold, hard cash all the way.

Let me elaborate. Have you ever stopped to ask why the Japanese market continues to get so much attention? Because it once went up a lot, that's why. (This statement is at the top of my "more profound than it looks" list for this book.) The Nikkei Dow is under 14,000 as I write these words, and I still see professional investors pining for the days of the late 1980s when it was above 40,000. The same principle applies to gold, even though its heyday was even longer ago. The halo of former good times is extremely powerful. It compares to the aura we might reserve for a former Wimbledon champion, a Bjorn Borg perhaps. But at least we sports fans have the common sense to know that Borg isn't going to win Wimbledon again. Sentimental investors are so blinded by the halo that they somehow believe that history will repeat itself—which, conveniently, makes selling unnecessary. If only they recognized that the real attachment is to the money that once was, they'd never take the fatal step of transferring that attachment to the company, market, or commodity whose good times made that money possible.

GAME PLAN

We've all heard of stocks that are hedges against inflation or even hedges against rising interest rates. Well, the sentimentalist should consider a different type of hedge, which begins by buying stocks that might have previously been repellent. Suppose you were managing a stock portfolio for the owner of a hardware store. Wouldn't you put Home Depot in the portfolio? It's as good a hedge as you can find. If the day comes when the store has to be shut down because of ravenous competition, you'd at least be participating in that competition the whole time. If Home Depot had been in the portfolio since the mid-1980s, it would take some mighty bad selections not to come out well ahead.

Of course, unless the portfolio was a blind trust, you might never have gotten Home Depot into it in the first place. And you might not want to see the look on your client's face upon finding out the source of his riches. But Home Depot was the perfect hedge, and it illustrates that sentimentalists can be better off if they learn to embrace on the investment side the very developments they resist in their daily life.

So go ahead. Buy something you can't stand. Go to the annual meeting. Try to put a human face on whatever trend seems so objectionable from afar. My guess is that an honest effort to confront the unconfrontable will be surprisingly easy. Remember that Sam Walton was himself a neighborhood five-and-dime retailer until he saw a better way. If you had gone to a Wal-Mart meeting when Sam was still alive, you'd have seen the corporate facade quickly melt away to reveal the homespun core.

And even if that approach doesn't work, you have the fallback option of becoming an activist shareholder, always there as a thorn in management's side to make sure they play by whatever rules you hold dear. There is no holding back progress, but there is something to be said for ushering it in in the right way.

On a different note, if you still find yourself making excuses not to sell when your inside knows otherwise, try creating your own "tax-adjusted" portfolio statement. (I first proposed this idea in Fidelity's "Independent Investor" newsletter back in 1989. Correct me if I'm wrong, but I don't believe it created a major stir among the nation's investment planners.) The idea is to counteract any faulty tax-based selling by carrying a face value and an estimated tax-adjusted liquidation value for each of your stock holdings. Creating a tax-adjusted portfolio would result in a one-time "hit" to your net worth, reflecting the fact that you never were as wealthy as you thought; that is, the tax burden was always there, even if your prior statement ignored it. The benefit is that once you got over the one-time hit, you could at least have a chance at making your investment decisions without the tax cloud interfering.

I should warn you that breaking through personal defenses is very tricky business. Defenses are at the same time extremely silly and extremely vital to our survival. If you like blaming your bad nonsell decisions on the infernal U.S. tax code, a tax-adjusted brokerage statement is a lousy idea. But doing nothing to counteract a known investment problem is an even worse idea. So tread carefully by all means, but if you've been burned by holding stocks too long, you have all the incentive you need to examine that practice and, ideally, to bring it to an end.

 # Personality Spotlight

Loyalty

Loyalty is a trait that is almost universally appreciated in real life, and one that a sentimentalist probably takes for granted when it comes to investments. However, when we encounter the trader and the adventurist personality types in later chapters, we will see that not everyone feels the same way about loyalty on the exchange floor, often for good reason.

Is it possible to value loyalty but not get burned by it? In the personality spotlight that accompanied the visionary chapter, I advised that a control freak might want to become more of a participatory investor by attending annual meetings and the like; I echoed those comments within this chapter for those sentimentalists whose problem is not being willing to invest in new ideas. But this same practice is *not* recommended for the sentimentalist whose problem is holding on to the old stocks too long, particularly when it comes to smaller companies.

Remember, the sentimentalist has a difficult time extricating himself or herself from a company that is foundering. Guilt often takes center stage at these moments because the sentimentalist views selling the stock as akin to the captain sneaking into a lifeboat. When enshrouded by guilt, you'll start to worry that someone will actually notice your absence from the meeting, your unreturned proxies, or any other signs of disentanglement. To the extent that these phantom worries get in the way of the selling process, get rid of them. Don't keep a file of old annual reports because they'll start looking like your children's old teddy bears. Anything you can do to maintain objectivity will improve your investment decisions.

Ultimately, we have to realize that the cherished attribution of loyalty is as semantically charged as many other adjectives we're looking at in this book. After all, *anyone* can be loyal when nothing is wrong, so true loyalty must imply sticking with something despite the problems it might have, as in a troubled marriage. But society has come to understand that while working to fix a marriage is admirable, staying in a doomed one is not. Perhaps that should be the working definition of *loyalty* for a sentimental investor.

"When you say Merrill, Lynch, Pierce, Fenner & Beane recommend a certain stock, do you mean it's unanimous or just a simple majority?"

THE
SKEPTIC

There are two types of skeptics in life: those who know too much, and those who know too little. The woman in the dated but somehow timeless Whitney Darrow cartoon could be in either category, depending on how you wish to read her facial expression. That's what makes the skeptic a special challenge to analyze. There may be a world of difference between the know-it-alls and the know-very-littles, but the two groups can look very much alike in the short run.

Imagine that you are invited to a swank dinner party for the upwardly mobile. There you are, enjoying yourself to no end, when the serenity of your evening is shattered by someone asking you to comment on the chardonnay being served with the main course. If your knowledge and taste buds are up to the challenge, you can certainly draw upon that background and give the wine a so-so review, if appropriate. No problem there. But if you had no knowledge whatsoever,

ARE YOU A SKEPTIC?

Answer these questions and find out:

1 When you get an envelope in the mail stating that you have won $10 million, does your pulse rise before reality sets in?

Even a minuscule pulse rise might disqualify you from true skepticdom.

2 Mark Twain said, "Anyone under 40 who is a pessimist knows too much. Anyone over 40 who is an optimist knows too little." Do you agree?

If the second part of the quotation rings truer than the first, this chapter may be for you.

3 Were you laughed at in first grade when you made a mistake in front of the class?

Not all skeptics were launched this way, but there's nothing like childhood trauma to clam us up for the rest of our lives. Letting other people voice their opinions and shooting them down is a way to atone for that early humiliation.

4 Do you take satisfaction in the knowledge that missing a good stock doesn't cost a penny, whereas investing in a bad stock can cost plenty?

The skeptic's mantra, and there's nothing wrong with it . . . in moderation.

5 Does your idea of stock market success demand a 70 percent accuracy rate?

You may want to recalibrate. Skeptics are apt to set their standards unrealistically high because the negative feelings from the losses outweigh the positive feelings from the gains, even if the net performance is still positive.

mightn't your response be the same? Where subjective judgments are concerned, those who take a negative view will always appear more sophisticated. Skepticism looks smart.

No one wants to look stupid where money is concerned, and the stock market can be every bit as subjective as a wine tasting—especially at the decision-making moments, when there is nobody who can declare you right or wrong. Over the long haul, that subjectivity eventually yields to the cold reality of performance numbers, so you'd think the know-nothing skeptic would be exposed. But even then, the passage of time can be surprisingly forgiving, and the skeptic who gets proved wrong will inevitably cope better with a simple shrug of the shoulders than will the defrocked optimist. That's the basic trap that afflicts this group of investors, and it's a powerful one. So, as we did with sentimentalists, we'll start with the negatives that await the hardened skeptic in pursuit of market riches.

PITFALLS

Too much of a good thing is a problem for anyone. You can't make money by *avoiding* stocks, and skeptics often relegate themselves to the sidelines as other, more optimistic types are doing awfully well. To see how this works in real life, let's roll the clock back to late 1990, to a company called Countrywide Credit.

Countrywide is the nation's leading independent mortgage broker, but its performance was anything but leading as the country lurched into recession in 1990. A quick pickup in inflation was making investors fearful of higher interest rates, which in turn could cause the mortgage refinancing market to dry up. On those fears, Countrywide stock plummeted 40 percent, to a 52-week low of $6 per share. (The chart on page 90 reflects subsequent stock splits, so it indicates a different 1990 low point.)

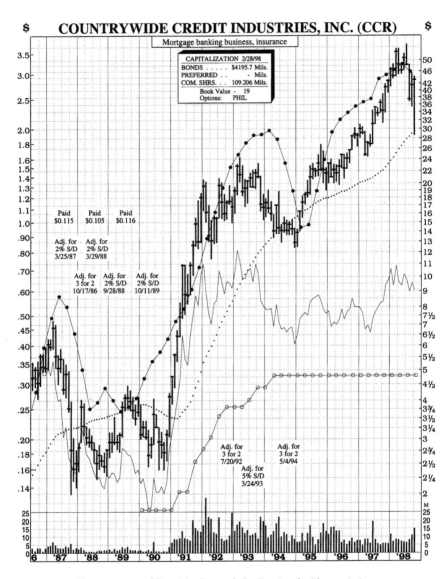

Chart courtesy of Securities Research Co. Reprinted with permission.

But not everyone was willing to throw in the towel. I had the good fortune to stumble across a recommendation of Countrywide by an analyst named Sy Jacobs, then of Morgan Keegan. The recommendation closed with a tantalizing scenario that Jacobs referred to as a "wildly bullish thought." The scenario was pretty much as follows: (1) Interest rates would reverse their trend and decline significantly over the next couple of years; (2) Countrywide would increase its share of the mortgage origination market; and (3) The stock market would value Countrywide's earnings stream as generously as it had during the good times of the past. In this three-pronged setting, Jacobs showed that the stock could easily increase more than fivefold.

To a skeptic, however, a "wildly bullish thought" is the earmark of an amateur and has no place in serious investing. Instead of buying the stock, the skeptic's wheels begin turning and a whole rash of objections emerges—as in, "Who said interest rates are going to come down three percentage points?" or "Didn't refinancing go out with the eighties?" and "Why should Countrywide increase its share, anyway?"

Well, guess what? Everything that seemed wildly bullish came true, and then some. The two years that followed were the most dynamic in Countrywide's history and helped fuel a *sevenfold* gain in the company's stock in just 18 months. The most enthusiastic analyst on the street had in fact erred on the downside. But the terminal skeptic would have missed out: So intent on dismissing the very notion of a wildly bullish hypothesis, the skeptic would have been blind to just what a bonanza was in store if that hypothesis came to pass.

The most cynical skeptics would have been suspicious of the Countrywide report from the mere fact that it came from a brokerage firm. The basic gripe is that brokerages issue far too many buy recommendations and far too few sell recommendations. That's not entirely a bum rap because there is a fundamental asymmetry between the words *buy* and *sell*. If an analyst says "buy," the stock in question can theoretically be acted on by any and all clients of the firm. If the analyst says "sell," however, the "pool of relevance" (just coined that expression) automatically shrinks to that much smaller group of people who happen to own the stock in the first place. Assuming that a stockbroker's ultimate goal is to generate commissions, you can see where the preference might lie.

Whether the imbalance between buy and sell recommendations should be *objectionable* is another matter. I first heard those objections when I started in the investment business in late 1982, at which time the Dow Jones Industrial Average was just crossing the 1000 barrier. Fifteen years later, the Dow had burst through 9000. Throughout that time, believe it or not, analysts were criticized for saying "buy" too often.

To the skeptic, the most dubious buy recommendations are those that come from a brokerage analyst whose firm also has an underwriting relationship with the client: namely, the company whose stock is being recommended. This objection makes more sense. First of all, not all brokerages are equally trustworthy, and unless you've forgotten about Drexel Burnham Lambert, you know that the zeal for underwriting revenues can mean dabbling with low-quality companies. Second, the notion that one arm of a brokerage firm could bring a company public and another arm could give an entirely objective view of that same company contradicts virtually any lesson any of us have ever learned about corporate cultures. It's an unwritten rule that analysts don't dump on their own firm's offerings, and we have every right to be suspicious. As the immortal Louis Zitnik wrote in the *Financial Analyst's Journal* in 1966, "Perhaps the greatest abuses in research reports occur in failure to discuss adequately the negatives in a situation (the sins of omission)."

Regarding the underwriting/recommendation tie-in, I have to confess that the first great stock I ever owned made itself known to me via a brokerage report, one that came my way via a mistake in the corporate mailroom. The report was written by a fellow at PaineWebber named Tom Caraisco. The company under discussion was shoe-and-clothing manufacturer Cherokee Group, which PaineWebber had brought public just months earlier. Caraisco's report noted that Cherokee had a 20 percent growth rate. The stock, then at $7^3/_4$, was trading at a preposterously low four times earnings. Remember the old warning not to pick up a $20 bill from the sidewalk? (If the bill was real, someone else would have gotten to it first.) Well, I was too naive to listen to warnings, and I was also too naive to worry about incidental brokerage connections. The information in the report was sound, and so was the result. Cherokee soared to $100 a share within a few short years.

I suppose the moral is that as long as you trust your ability to listen to the facts behind a recommendation as opposed to the bubbly enthusiasm that might accompany it, the source shouldn't matter all that much. But perhaps the best argument not to entirely dismiss post-IPO recommendations is that all of history's great stocks were brought public by *someone*.

Personalitywise, the subject of brokerage recommendations reveals an enormous gap between the skeptics and the contrarians, two groups that might appear to spring from the same curmudgeonly crowd. The contrarian loves a stock that is undiscovered, and if only one analyst is writing reports on the company, so much the better. But that first analyst is invariably from the underwriting firm, making the stock all but off-limits to the skeptic.

BRIGHT SPOTS

By all this I don't want to imply that skeptics can't make money in the stock market, because they can. The skeptic who doesn't like *anything* is actually a caricature. In real life, all but the most embittered investors have their likes as well as their dislikes. For example, skeptics would have an easier time than contrarians in buying the Johnson & Johnsons and the American Expresses of the world. A nice, conservative portfolio is perfect because what it lacks in imagination can easily be made up for in comfort, stability, and even results.

Where a knowledgeable skeptic has a big advantage over the rest of the crowd is in identifying those companies whose seemingly outstanding results are in fact a by-product of creative accounting. Generally accepted accounting principles (GAAP) allow for more latitude than the nonskeptic would ever believe, and in the extreme they can provide the noose with which a company hangs itself and its shareholders.

I should admit that when I entered the investment business, I was surprised that accounting tomfoolery was as widespread as it was. I thought the necessary safeguards were in place in the form of constant reviews by auditors, to say nothing of the omnipresent Securities and Exchange Commission (SEC). Even more to the point, I couldn't imagine that company managements would play accounting games that were surely doomed to failure. One early piece of evidence to the contrary was the collapse of piano maker turned insurance conglomerate Baldwin-United in 1983. I read in awe as the *Wall Street Journal* chronicled the investigative research of young analyst Jim Chanos, who unmasked the company's shameless reshuffling of assets that was somehow passed off as earnings growth.

In 1986, when quick-oil-change franchisor Jiffy Lube came public, I was one of hundreds who attended the Boston road show. Amid the dozens of cream-puff questions that were lofted at company management, it took hyperaggressive fund manager Ken Heebner to break the mood with one biting question: "How do you prevent franchisees from cheating?" Gulp. What no one knew at the time was that Jiffy Lube would soon cheat on its own income statement by prematurely logging "area development rights"—in effect, recognizing revenues they had yet to earn. Once this practice was exposed, the accounting restatement created a loss in 1989 of $79 million, compared with an apparent profit of $7 million in 1988. The stock lost almost all of its value between 1987 and 1990.

So why do companies do such things when disaster awaits? Howard Schilit, accounting professor turned corporate sleuth and author of *Financial Shenanigans,* notes three primary reasons: (1) It pays to do it; (2) It's easy to do; and (3) It's unlikely you'll get caught. Soberingly, the task of identifying any and all shenanigans is dumped squarely on the common stock investor's lap because they're the point of last resort. One of the major carrot sticks for fraudulent financial reporting lies in the riches from taking a company public, and no one in the chain, from company executives to auditors to underwriting firms, has a financial incentive to put on the brakes.

Even when you feel that a company's management is guilty of nothing more than optimism, accounting irregularities can still shoot an investment to hell. My favorite example is Lorimar, the television studio best known for producing the perennially high-rated prime time soap operas *Dallas, Knot's Landing,* and *Falcon Crest.* As the popularity of these series skyrocketed in the early 1980s, Lorimar could reasonably contemplate a successful syndication for any or all of them. On these hopes, the stock moved from under $10 per share in 1981 to over $25 by mid-1984.

These gains notwithstanding, a skeptic would have noticed that studios such as Lorimar don't actually reel in a lot of cash during the early years of a series. The studios are compensated at below production costs by the networks, a situation that is tolerable only because of the everpresent hope of hitting it big in the syndication market. The key accounting issue is this: Expenses are matched against revenues, and as the likelihood of a successful syndication increases, GAAP allows a studio to postpone some of its production costs so as to smooth out the earnings stream. There is nothing illegal in this approach; but clearly if the syndication isn't as lucrative as hoped, the studio not only suffers a shortfall at that time, it must also restate years of inflated earnings results because the actual costs of producing the series had been understated. That specific irregularity was unearthed in the due diligence review that accompanied Lorimar's merger with Telepictures in 1986. The stock of the merged company fell from its high of $32 to just $8 in little more than a year.

The teensy-weensy problem for those who specialize in identifying negatives such as these is what we've already seen: Money isn't made by avoiding stocks; it's made by taking some sort of action. Putting two and two together, it makes sense to investigate the short side of the Street.

It is natural to think that a skeptic could be retrained to excel by selling stocks short—thereby profiting from the declines they seem to foresee in every corner. Although I won't go into the precise mechanics of how to sell a stock short, suffice it to say that the process involves "borrowing" shares from your broker in hopes of buying them back at a lower price. If the stock continues upward instead, you face an essentially unlimited liability, which is one reason why so many are skeptical of the shorting practice itself!

I find myself reminded of Democratic congressman Barney Frank's disgust a few years back as he saw his own party pandering to one special interest group or another. When fellow Democrats finally showed greater resolve, Frank, far from exulting, instead drolly pointed out, "Now we're pandering to the antipanderers." I can only add that simultaneous aversion to *both sides* of the stock market game, short and long, is a good sign that skepticism has gone too far.

For those who do want to test the waters of short-selling, opportunity abounds, but one simple piece of advice is to distinguish reflexive skepticism (this stock is just plain too high) from analytical skepticism (this company is inflating its revenues). As we saw in the Polaroid and Avon examples in the introduction, there is nothing to prevent an already overpriced stock from becoming even more overpriced. When that happens, the short seller faces the ugly prospect of losses that are every bit as unlimited as the stock's ability to climb. By contrast, when Wall Street finally recognizes a fundamental accounting problem, the stock can be underwater indefinitely, possibly permanently.

As simple as the foregoing advice sounds, inexperienced short-sellers consistently overlook it because it is sexier to catch the current high-flier—when there is still a chance to short at the absolute top—than it is to short a stock that has already begun to fall. This is where an utter disregard for the efficient market theory comes in awfully handy. When a company is truly troubled (Jiffy Lube, 1989; LA Gear, 1991; Kaypro, 1985; First Executive, 1989; Lomas Financial, 1993; etc.), the share price can grind down for years before it can grind down no more. There is plenty of time to place your short.

Speaking of time, the final point I'd like to make about short selling is that the name itself provides a valuable strategic clue. If you are "short" a stock, you have sold borrowed shares; this is in contrast to being "long" a stock, which is trader's parlance for owning it. And just as ownership is primarily a long-term affair, the preferred time horizon for most short sales is, you guessed it, short. After all, if you're asking that a stock diverge from the market's long-term uptrend, you may be pushing your luck to ask for an extended divergence. And who's to say that the company won't fix the problem that made you so pessimistic in the first place? The "dream" short sales of the prior paragraph are exceptions on both counts.

In general, whereas long-term shareholders suffer only paper losses if their investments temporarily reverse themselves, short sellers face the dreaded prospect of "margin calls"—reminders from your broker that the collateral on your loan has dwindled, forcing you to cough up more money. The cost of having your capital tied up in this fashion provides the short seller with yet more incentive to act *after* a company has revealed weakness (in the tip of the iceberg sense, of course), as opposed to shorting and waiting for the weakness you deem inevitable to occur in the first place. Godot might seem punctual by comparison.

GAME PLAN

Some years ago, Charles D. Ellis of Greenwich Associates came out with an article entitled "The Loser's Game," a concept that garnered a fair amount of attention. Ellis's point was that the stock market resembles a game like clay court tennis, in that the winner is almost always the person who makes the fewest number of mistakes. Avoid the mistakes and you'll come out ahead.

I have to wonder how many of today's skeptics were influenced by that line of thinking. The wrinkle is that Ellis wrote his article in 1981, a time when the financial markets had yet to break out from a multiyear funk. As we know, the market's subsequent behavior has made a mockery of the "loser's game" approach. If anything, the market has resembled *grass court* tennis, because the advantages have accrued to the aggressor, not to the person unwilling to make the first mistake.

It's easy to be critical of Ellis's advice, but in trying to carve out some timeless advice for the skeptical crowd, I had best recognize that I am also a prisoner of my times. This book was conceived in the afterglow of an extended bull market. So if you felt that skeptics were given a tough time in the chapter just finished, you're probably right.

To those skeptics who truly felt left out of the market's party, I would suggest reviewing those investments you decided to pass on

and analyzing why your decision was made the way it was. Did you re-
flexively think that the company's good fortune couldn't continue? That
puts you squarely in the "didn't know enough" mode. I can't count the
number of times in my investment career that I have seen optimism on
a stock emanating from the very same institutional portfolio managers
who were pessimistic just months or weeks before. In the interim, they
acquired that precious commodity called knowledge.

If you're one of those who said "no" because you found something about the company you didn't like—but still missed out—it's time
to reassess whether that blemish was really a decisive negative or
whether it was just an excuse not to buy. All too often, skeptics fix-
ate on a particular blemish a company might have (and they all have
them), only to find that the one imperfection didn't affect the core of
the company's success.

The issue of bogus accounting is the one area where we could all
be more skeptical. One of the reasons why naivete is so widespread is
that we tend to take reported earnings per share at face value. The
daily newspaper does not typically take the time to outline a company's key accounting assumptions; and even if it did, we might not
appreciate their power.

But if you've ever made a mistake on your income taxes (you
have, haven't you?), you are in a position to understand the potential
fragility of corporate earnings. The bonus check you forgot to include,
the deductible donation you accidentally double-counted, the mistake
you made in calculating depreciation—whatever the underlying cause,
it can transform a refund into a liability. Corporate accounting is no
different, except that the line items are about a hundred times more
numerous.

So when a company says it earned $1.12 per share in the most re-
cent quarter, you owe it to yourself to find out where the money actually came from. The greater your comfort with the quality of earnings,
the greater your peace of mind with the stock. That's the type of skepticism that everyone would do well to acquire.

Personality Spotlight

Perfectionism

The perfectionist isn't the only skeptic in town, but many people who turn down one stock after another do so because they are waiting for the perfect one to show up. Sort of like waiting for Mister Right, and equally futile. Perfectionists must adjust to the fact that the stock market is a highly imperfect place. It's almost unimaginable that a stock will ever come around that has every single ingredient they'd like. To me, a perfect stock is one that goes up half a point every single day. Too bad that I've just ruled out every public company that has ever been.

As we all know, you don't have to be right all of the time in order to make money in the stock market. Some traders claim that they'll come out ahead with a success ratio as low as 51 percent. And surely once you get in the 70 percent range, you're almost certainly talking about some very handsome returns.

Amazingly the perfectionist will find it extremely difficult to live with a success ratio *as low as* 70 percent. Never mind the ever-present parallel to baseball, where anything over 30 percent makes for an extremely successful hitter and 40 percent can only be dreamed about. The perfectionist discards such parallels because in investing, there is no one throwing 90-mile-per-hour fastballs at you. The hitter has an excuse for not succeeding all the time. The investor does not.

There are two possible outcomes of this stance, and neither is very good. The first possibility is that the perfectionist investor does pretty well, but the investment returns are arguably no match for the misery endured in attaining them. The second and worse possibility is that the investor becomes so disgusted with a 60 percent success ratio that he or she gets frustrated and takes wild actions to try and make up for that woeful performance. Alas, the paradoxical result is that the success ratio doesn't even reach the 60 percent standard that was deemed so inadequate in the first place.

The market has never been perfect, and it's hard to imagine what it would look like if it were. If you're a perfectionist at heart, find some other outlet for your trait and give your investments some slack. You just might be happy with the result.

B. Smaller

"Up a hundred and sixteen points! If only we'd had the
foresight to invest ten minutes ago."

THE
TRADER

We all know what traders do. They maneuver and shuffle their holdings in hopes of short-term profits. Did they never get the word that long-term investing is the way to go? Well, many don't believe it, or even if they do believe it, they can't bear to stay out of the action.

In this chapter, I'm going to keep my promise of withholding judgment about what is right and what is wrong, other than to say that it is quite arguably wrong to tell someone to make only long-term investments when their psychological makeup doesn't permit it. Would you force your ADD grandchild to sit through *La Traviata?* Our job as investors is to do the best we can with what we've got. Besides, there's probably a bit of trader mentality in anyone who diligently follows the markets, even those who aren't piling up transactions every day. So even if you recoil from the "trader" label, this chapter may be for you.

BRIGHT SPOTS

The first bright spot for the trader is admittedly a hypothetical one: Namely, if you are willing to suppose that the person who constantly

ARE YOU A TRADER?

Answer these questions and find out:

1 How many times per year do you *not* know the closing market numbers by the time you have dinner?

> *If the answer is "five or fewer," you just might have the market addiction that will make this chapter relevant.*

2 Do you ever "fight the tape" (as in, hold on to something that's going down, or sell something that's going up)?

> *Traders like action, but most would answer "no." When a stock is going down, they assume someone else knows the bad news, even if they don't.*

3 Do you read two or more newspapers per day?

> *Traders don't like to be left out. If they aren't news junkies, they've got something else to absorb themselves in.*

4 Do you cringe when the newspaper reveals a stock that got away from you?

> *Traders especially don't like to be left out of that sort of thing, and they can't muster the equanimity that a long-term investor might.*

5 Are you self-confident?

> *If not, then you can at least be confident that you don't need to read this chapter.*

watches the market is better positioned to know when certain stocks are trading unusually cheaply, then you have to acknowledge that these investors have an advantage based on pure arithmetic. If you or I buy a stock at $25 and watch it go to $30, we're up 20 percent for our efforts. If a vigilant trader spots an intraday dip and is able to buy at $20, that same move to $30 is now worth 50 percent.

More generally, if a market session is unusually volatile, it may create opportunities that the average investor will never be able to exploit. For example, on August 31, 1998, the Dow Jones Industrial Average plunged over 500 points. The next morning there was continued weakness but then a sharp reversal: Home Depot, to name one, traded as low as 35 but then rebounded to 41. That's nearly a 20 percent return, all in the space of four hours.

The problem with these bright spots, of course, is that they represent merely one direction in a street that we know to be two-way. Who's to say that you will get better prices just by vigilance? And who's to say that you can't get slaughtered on a volatile day by overactive trading? For all we know, those Home Depot "investors" were just winning back the money they had lost the day before. Clearly we need to add a little bit of structure before we accord traders a permanent advantage over the rest of us.

Getting Technical

If you don't believe that active traders can get consistently good prices for their stocks, you might be interested to know that there is a whole class of market devotees who thrive by getting *worse* prices than you or I might. They're called technical analysts. Let me explain: With some risk of oversimplification, a technical analyst, also known as a technician or a chartist, is one who believes that a good stock can be distinguished from a bad stock on the basis of its price history alone. The technician's classic approach is to let other people worry about a company's inventory levels, its competitive prospects, and sometimes even the absolute valuation level of its stock. The idea is that all of those factors have been blended by other market participants to create the price history that forms the chart. Everything is connected, or so goes the theory, and in that sense the technician is the stock market's version of the iridologist—you know, the doctor who looks into your eyeball and tells you that your liver is failing.

Implicitly, a chartist believes that a chart that looks like the one on page 107 is more likely to go on to look like the chart on page 108 than like the final chart on page 109.

Because chartists believe in momentum, they will often wait for a stock to go up before buying and wait for a downturn before selling—that's what I meant by saying they get worse prices than you or I. This strategy sounds pretty dumb until you consider that all of history's great stocks started by going up enough to appear on the chartists' ever-vigilant, momentum-detecting radar screens, and all of the great disasters first fell a worrisome amount before they collapsed altogether. When dealing with stocks whose price movements are extreme enough, you can beat the market handily even without pinpoint timing.

There is more to the technician's craft, of course: Spend enough time with this crowd and you'll hear talk of "resistance levels," "support levels," and other acknowledgments that stocks move in two directions. But it is fair to say that technicians aren't known for fighting the tape, a stance that places them diametrically opposite the contrarian. Contrarians are stubborn and have the constitution to hold through thick and thin, whereas technicians can be as fickle as a Hollywood agent. Contrarians buy early and sometimes sell early. Technicians are happy to buy late and sometimes sell late, in the hope that the in-between payoff will more than compensate them for their troubles.

Above all, traders are set apart from most long-term investors because their clocks are calibrated differently; traders not only care about what they own, they care deeply about *when* they own it. As a case in point, I remember an amusing *Smart Money* article written in 1994 by the ubiquitous hedge fund manager James Cramer, who would go on to found TheStreet.com and thereby become the mouthpiece for a generation of high-octane investors. Cramer acknowledged that he was "dying to own Intel" and that he would punch the ticker symbol five or ten times

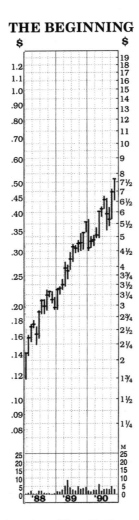

Chart courtesy of Securities Research Co.
Reprinted with permission.

a day to make sure it wasn't getting away from him. So why didn't he spare himself the angst and just buy the damn thing? Because he wasn't comfortable with the circumstances of the moment. The overall market was behaving erratically. Intel itself was between product lines, and when they did get around to launching the ballyhooed Pentium chip late that year, they faced a public relations crisis and a major stock market ripple

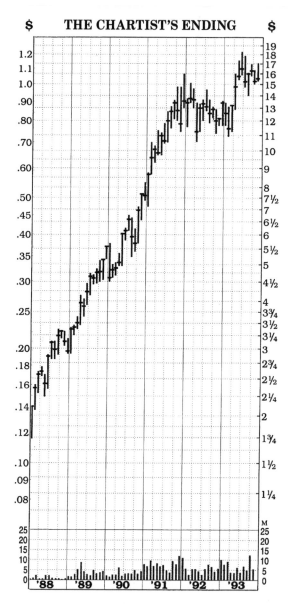

$ THE CHARTIST'S ENDING $

Chart courtesy of Securities Research Co. Reprinted with permission.

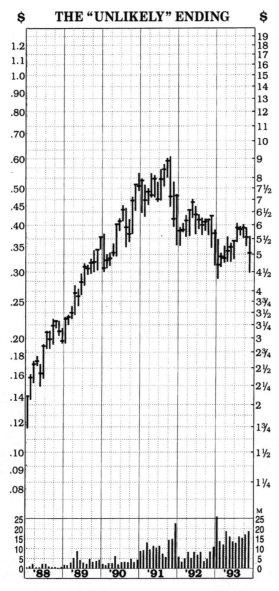

Chart courtesy of Securities Research Co. Reprinted with permission.

when the chip didn't calculate properly. It took a full year before everything took off in the right direction: not much time as long-term investments go, but that's 7 dog years and perhaps 15 trader years. Intel shares quintupled between 1995 and 1997, and you can bet your bottom dollar that Cramer was riding the wave.

Flexibility

As the Intel example shows, one of the biggest advantages possessed by many traders is their flexibility. But in order to establish flexibility as a bona fide advantage, we first have to address the fact that not all investors feel that *in*flexibility is such a terrible thing.

For starters, recall that the Graham and Dodd school of value investing is based on a completely rigid model: Buy when a stock trades below "net current assets," sell when it has gone up 50 percent, and so forth. Nowadays you won't find many stocks that satisfy those original purchase criteria, but to the extent that today's bargain hunters are really the stock market stepchildren of Graham and Dodd, structure and rigidity have forged a good reputation.

This reputation is enhanced by the attention accorded such strategies as *dollar-cost averaging,* whose adherents follow a plan of investing equal dollar sums across equal time intervals. The scheme is inflexible, but that's the whole point. Done properly, dollar-cost averaging can neutralize market fluctuations, in that a fixed number of dollars will automatically buy more shares when prices are low and fewer shares when prices are high.

If all this weren't enough, inflexibility gets a further push by the example set by successful blackjack players, all of whom would surely fail unless they followed their "system," whatever that might be. The operative word behind all of these strategies is *discipline,* a quality that no investor should be without.

However, discipline is one thing and inflexibility quite another. Flexible investors have a very specific advantage because in the parlance of this book, they are able to avoid that investment scourge known as the *implanted idea*. Suppose you owned Nike back in 1983, as the company was enduring a difficult transitional stage following its successful public offering. Maybe you lost confidence and sold. No problem with that; you're human. But would you have been able to get back in a few years later, when Nike was on the verge of becoming an international powerhouse? For most of us, that prior experience might have eliminated Nike from the radar screen altogether, which is why the question "Would you be willing to get back in to a stock that had disappointed you before?" is such a great litmus test for flexibility.

My search for a truly flexible investor ended when I called upon Dave Cameron, manager of the "Short/Long" mutual fund for the investment firm Standish, Ayer & Wood. Dave's fund is unique not only because it is *market neutral* (he holds both long and short positions), but also because it relies on a computer-driven discipline that encourages flexibility rather than rigidity. Time and again, Cameron's model has alerted him to buying opportunities that blissfully disregarded any prior experience he might have had with the stock.

Cameron's on-again, off-again ownership of Carnival Cruise Lines is an instructive case history: He started buying Carnival in late 1991 at about $12 per share. The investment was a trial balloon, on the order of one-half of 1 percent of the entire portfolio, because it was really his computer's idea, not his. He admitted, "I didn't really have a handle on the company's fundamentals and how they were able to generate the numbers they did." As a result of this uncertainty, Cameron decided to take a profit in April 1993 at $17 per share. But the computer didn't forget: Another system-prompted trial balloon was launched in November 1994, with that position being sold the next year at a slight loss.

It wasn't until September 1995 that Cameron finally had the confidence to invest again—for the long haul. By that time he had developed an understanding of just how well the folks at Carnival executed their basic business. They knew how and when to adjust pricing levels to maximize revenues for each and every cruise. Their outstanding service generated a tremendous amount of repeat business. They kept on making acquisitions and bringing on new ships, notably Cunard and its *QEII*. Cameron bought in at $23, a higher price than his prior selling price but still a great success, because by late 1997 the stock was at $54—unadjusted for an interim 2-for-1 split, for comparison purposes. Then, in the aftermath of the movie *Titanic,* the cruise business was positively flying (an odd reaction, given the *Titanic's* real-life fate, but poetic justice, in that another Cameron—James—directed the film). Bookings and pricing levels at Carnival were stronger than ever, and by mid-1998 the stock reached $85.

If you as a long-term investor feel obliged to point out that Cameron would have been better off had he simply bought at $12 in 1991 and held on, you're absolutely right. He'd even agree with you. His trading record on the stock looks wishy-washy from afar. But to be able to return to a discarded stock is a characteristic that all investors would do well do cultivate. It is a sign that when future opportunities arise, you will be able to analyze them thoroughly and objectively, and that alone puts you ahead of the game. All too often, investors say, "I can always get back in later," when they're really just trying to make themselves feel better about jettisoning a stock whose behavior has them spooked. Maintaining a fine balance of flexibility—with rigidity to one side and wishy-washiness to the other—is the hallmark of a superior investor.

Let me close this section by mentioning that the first conversation I ever had with Dave Cameron concerned his rationale for shorting Apple Computer in 1993 (a great investment move if ever one was). I have already cited the Apple saga a couple of times in the book, and Mac devotees might have taken offense at my failure to acknowledge that the company staged an impressive rebound beginning with the return of Steve Jobs in 1997. Well, the most recent phone conversation I had with Dave Cameron came early in Jobs's second tenure, and as we reminisced about his prior great short, he disappeared momentarily into his databases and finally said, "You know, Apple is looking more and more like a buy right now." That's flexibility for you.

PITFALLS

The trader is uniquely vulnerable to a nasty phenomenon known as the "whipsaw." That's when you buy at $45, sell at $40, and watch from the sidelines as the stock then hits $60. "I had the right idea. I just got whipsawed." All I can say is that frequent whipsaws either mean you've been horribly unlucky or you don't know what you're doing. The more times you try to outsmart the near-term market, the more times you'll face this problem.

Speaking of outsmarting, another problem faced by the trader is also familiar to the contrarian, which is being too clever for your own good. When you're in the market every day, it's surprisingly easy to get lured into extremely risky positions. And getting hammered by being short Malaysia at the wrong time is not only a financial problem, it's a psychological one. It's downright embarrassing to lose money on some obscure currency while your grandmother is sitting on her Johnson & Johnson and beating the pants off of you. Before you get into such transactions, think: Do I really feel confident that the peso is going to lose ground to the ringgit, or have I lost perspective entirely?

My eternal alphabetic companion, Victor Niederhoffer, became a celebrated victim of a Far East trading snafu in mid-1997. Worse still, he compounded that error via a seemingly innocent options transaction that became catastrophic when the market had a one-day free fall a few months later. The particulars of the transaction aren't important, except to say that you could make a case that Niederhoffer was genuinely unlucky. He was betting on a rising market, and the S&P did in fact go on to hit record highs. On the other hand, his was a risk to which the aggressive short-term investor is uniquely vulnerable, even if it took a freak of nature to expose it. Short-term bets do not lend themselves to long-term solutions. The fact that the S&P soon made up all its lost ground was of no more consolation than the fact that a hurricane or a tornado doesn't stay long. Who cares? The damage was done.

Even without such cataclysms, let's not forget the most basic psychological pitfall of the trader: having to consistently take actions that are contrary to your emotions. It's easy to say that you buy when others are running scared, but when you place yourself squarely in the middle of the market's everyday life, who's to say that your emotions are any different? To make matters worse, the moment you pat yourself on the back for a purchase well made, you have to ask whether you need to sell. In this sense, the trader's psychological dilemma is very much akin to the contrarian's, except that it gets played out much more frequently. Is it any wonder that so many traders burn out quickly?

The final pitfall for the trader is on a more philosophical note. Does it really make sense to become a creature of the market and nothing else? Can you turn off the switch for those increasingly rare moments when the market isn't open, or does the market go on to dominate your entire life? No less an investor than Jeff Vinik admitted that when he managed the Magellan Fund, it was especially important for the fund to do well on Fridays because those were the results that he carried in his mind throughout the weekend. Fundholders who saw that comment might have been concerned that the fund wouldn't live up to its stated long-term goals. A psychologist might have been concerned that the fund manager was losing his mind.

It is no secret that long-term investors have traditionally felt themselves superior to traders and technical analysts of all types. Investors argue that they play an indispensable role by supplying the capital that is essential for the nation's economic development; traders, by contrast, are nothing but parasites of the vast market system, contributing absolutely zero in the way of social benefit.

My own experience is that the gulf between the two groups isn't nearly that great. Long-term investors may indeed supply the capital that drives the nation, but they are motivated by the desire to make money, just like our friends the traders. And it's hard to overlook George Soros, who made his billions on the trading floor and then became perhaps the biggest philanthropist in history. Is he less wholesome than the long-term investor? I am reminded of a comment made years ago by a hedge fund manager who lamented that what he did—making piles of money for people who didn't need it—was useless, but what was wrong with making a few million dollars a year as he decided what he wanted to do with his life? It was tough to argue with.

GAME PLAN

With this final pitfall in mind, it is axiomatic that to be a successful trader, you must feel comfortable with what you do. The worst combination is pursuing short-term trading while harboring some qualms about whether it truly suits your psyche, and ending up doing poorly in the process.

And if you decide that trading has some appeal, you might be gratified to know that long-term investors—the very group that looks down on you—can be financially penalized for their condescension. Sentimentalists are known to miss opportunities to take profits (or, for that matter, to get out of a stock whose fundamentals have changed for the worse) because selling prematurely makes them feel like the loathsome trader. Instead, they persist with a pitiful Prince Valiant imitation and hold on until the stock has caused them such emotional anguish that they punt, as if enduring pain and selling too late is an honorable way to invest. Those with a more normal pain threshold (that's you) will never suffer through this type of experience.

One of the best game plans for the trader is also a foreshadowing of how portfolios can be harnessed to accommodate wayward personality traits: "Keep any short-term trades separate from your long-term investments." This advice is not new. In fact, it is ripped off. Jim Cramer gave that very advice in a *Time* magazine column in 1998. On a practical level, the message is that it is perfectly reasonable to sell shares of American Express when they "feel" too high to you, even as you hold on to those same shares in your long-term account. There's no contradiction here. By following this dual approach, Cramer (and you) will simply own more of a stock when it appears attractive for both the short and the long terms and, ideally, less at interim peaks. The title of his column was "Trade or Invest?" As you can see, it is possible to do both.

Taking this process a step further, if you are a new investor and you think you have a trading mentality, why not place your short-term and long-term accounts in competition with one another? That way you can assuage your itch to act when a stock gets overpriced, all the while hedging against your own itchiness by investing long term, just the way you were taught. If it turns out that your short-term portfolio is ahead after five years or so, maybe you really do have the "right stuff" that justifies an even bigger commitment to a shorter-term investment style. And if it turns out otherwise, at least you found out through direct experience and not someone else's preaching. May the better investor win.

 # Personality Spotlight

Self-Consciousness

It may have occurred to you that most of the traders in the world aren't exactly the self-conscious type. If you have ever seen the classic snapshot of activity on the exchange floor, whether it be for stocks, currencies, or pork futures, you probably recognize that these people never gain through timidity. One assumes that the system weeds out anyone and everyone who lacks the constitution to hack the boisterous nature of the trading floor. You have to be self-confident, not self-conscious.

Self-conscious types are especially vulnerable to the perils of the buying moment as discussed in the introduction. If you don't like to have attention drawn to yourself, how in the world do you place your sell order? How do you explain to your broker why you're doing what you're doing? (Never mind that it isn't any of the broker's business, and that in fact the broker may not care. Self-conscious people don't understand these things. If they did, they wouldn't have their hang-ups in the first place.)

Despite these problems, I have good news for the self-conscious investor. First of all, you have company. You'd never think of Jeff Vinik, former manager of the Fidelity Magellan Fund, as being self-conscious, what with the constant interviews and public speaking engagements that were part of his job. He managed to farsightedly place a gigantic and controversial 40 percent of the fund's holdings in technology despite being watched by the whole world. Yet when he followed that move with an ill-fated and equally highly publicized foray into bonds, you couldn't help but think that he had capitulated to the unrelenting public fascination about what Vinik's next great move would be. (His bond move was actually something of a brilliant stroke, but it came way too early. And in the quarterly/daily mutual-fund-performance mindset, being early is the same as being wrong.)

The proof of this particular pudding was found when Vinik left Fidelity to run his own hedge fund. His performance for his very first year was 94 percent, 58 percentage points above the market and way higher than the solid but ultimately unspectacular results he chalked up while heading Magellan. This eye-popping performance was compelling evidence that Magellan had grown too big (indeed, the fund was soon closed to new investors) and that a smaller hedge fund was a better match for someone with Vinik's skill because he could place more concentrated bets. But perhaps his early investors also saw that he would benefit by being out of the limelight, free to do exactly what he pleased without constant second-guessing. And it certainly worked.

For the rest of us, technology has come to the rescue. For all the hub-bub about the convenience of online trading, you almost never hear of its important side effect—how liberating it is for the self-conscious investor. At long last, you don't have to explain your trades because you're dealing with a machine. The result is that self-conscious investors should never have to experience that nauseating sensation of holding on to a stock they have grown to dislike merely because they can't summon the gumption to make the telephone call that would relieve them of that responsibility.

One warning: If you happen to be a trader already, the convenience of online trading might be too much of a good thing. If it has converted you from a participant in the market to a prisoner of the market, you may want to take some time off.

"Don't you just <u>adore</u> it?"

THE
ADVENTURIST

The woman in the Peter Arno cartoon is obviously excited, but just what is the "it" that she adores? Is it the money she's won? Is it the thrill of placing a bet? To some people, there isn't all that much difference between the two experiences. In the immortal words of Nick the Greek, "The best thing in life is winning a bet. The second best thing is losing a bet." Such is life for the adventurist, who revels in putting everything on the line.

Of course, it is quite unfashionable to discuss the stock market with terms you might use at the racetrack or the casino. Society claims to have moved beyond that form of disparagement. But there are more speculators out there than you might imagine. In my days as an online columnist, I recommended all sorts of stocks; but even though I tried to be careful with my categorizations—as in distinguishing a growth stock from a value stock, a takeover candidate from a high-yielder, and so on—I discovered that the most popular selections by far were those

ARE YOU AN ADVENTURIST?

Answer these questions and find out:

1 Did you earn the money you're investing, or did you inherit it?

Some investors become adventurists because they don't really feel that the money is theirs, so they don't have the same reservations about risking it, for better or worse. Donald Trump and Malcolm Forbes are complicated variations on this theme.

2 Do you like bungee jumping?

Sorry, but adventurous activities such as bungee jumping or hang gliding don't necessarily translate into aggressive investing. Often these activities are undertaken by conservative people who want to step out of their personalities, and the same unpredictable element can apply to risk-taking investors.

3 Do you have a death wish?

This question melds the two that preceded it. Many adventurists spend their entire investment careers walking the line of self-destruction.

4 If your success ratio with IPOs, technology start-ups, and biotech companies is 50 percent, are you happy?

You probably should be delighted, because the half that went up presumably contributed a whole lot more than the half that went down. Even a lower success ratio might work out just fine, but not everyone has the stomach for it. Adventurists do.

5 Do you like talking about your various adventures?

One reason why adventurists make the investments they do is that making money by more conventional means doesn't create as interesting a story.

stocks I mentioned as rank speculations. Something about that description drove people absolutely wild.*

The reason this category is different boils down to associations. When we think of an adventurist, we think of a risk taker, and the very term carries the implication of a *reckless* risk taker—a gambler. After all, a successful risk taker would have to be called a visionary, right? If I wanted to, I could give the adventurist very little attention, as follows:

BRIGHT SPOTS

You can make a lot of money by speculating . . . as long as you're right.

PITFALLS

You can lose a lot of money if you're wrong.

I hope I can say something more meaningful before this chapter is over. But I'll admit that I'm not positioned to cure the compulsive gambler, whose problems extend well beyond the scope of this book. Nor can I address each and every individual adventurist's circumstance, as in the "irresponsible" heir or heiress whose adventurous investments represent a subconscious wish to make the money go away.

The reason the adventurist category is worth our attention is that it provides us with an excuse to discuss *risk,* a vital concept that to this point we've only tiptoed around. In theory, the world is divided into conservative (risk-averse) investors and aggressive (risk-taking) investors. So why didn't I create just those two personality types and

---

* I soon realized that I was doing a disservice by even mentioning these stocks. Readers inferred that what I really meant was that I had checked the story out and discovered it wasn't a speculation at all; what I did mean, of course, was that I had checked the story out and concluded that it remained completely speculative! Big difference, but the appeal of speculation lives on.

leave everything else alone? Because a brief examination of our first six personality categories reveals that risk isn't always what it seems.

Sentimentalists, for example, don't think of themselves as risk takers, yet time and again they hold on to companies that are well past their prime and find out through bitter experience just how risky these holdings are. Bargain hunters face similar problems, in that cheap stocks don't have to be good stocks. In particular, the market has a nasty habit of masking risks by making lousy companies tantalizingly cheap. Skeptics, meanwhile, go out of their way to avoid the loss of capital, and in that quest they are often successful. However, if their goal is to outperform the market, they can't achieve that objective without taking some sort of risk. It's no coincidence that Treasury bills can't match the stock market's returns over the long term.

On the other side of the risk coin, the contrarians, the visionaries, and the traders of the world are more commonly associated with risk taking. We saw that contrarians were drawn to down-and-out companies such as Chrysler or USAir, where the risks were *operational* in character, and that traders court *market* risk every trading session of the year, even when dealing solely with blue-chip stocks. But not all traders are adventurists. Arbitrageurs, for example, seek to exploit pricing inefficiencies in the market by using hedging strategies that are theoretically extremely low risk, even if they result in heavy trading volume. Visionaries can also fool you. In general, they invest not because they are eager to make an outlandish bet, but because their view of a rosy future is so clear that it obscures any risks involved in getting there. Together, our personality categories prove the vital point that risk is in the eye of the beholder.

A Beta Way?

Mathematically, the risk of an individual stock is often modeled by something called a *beta*. A stock's beta is computed by comparing the recent movement of the stock with that of the overall market, typically by plotting the stock's return versus the market's return at various intervals and creating something called a least-squares fit.

The idea behind this calculation is that a stock that goes up and down a lot (high beta) should be considered riskier than a stock whose oscillations are more dampened (low beta). In other words, if a stock goes from 40 to 80 by going up a quarter-point per day, that's much better than a stock that goes from 40 to 80 by going up 5 points one day, losing 4 the next, and so on. All other factors being equal, a steady rise is better because not only does it provide the same point-to-point return as the volatile stock, it also lets us know what we're getting if we have to sell at any time in between.

The beta concept is useful in the sense that different people react differently to the idea of something bobbing up and down. Perfectionists are irritated by such fluctuation and can make the mistake of taking it personally. Visionaries and other long-term investors can have an easier time with volatility, because they're looking out so far into the future that they don't even see it. Whoever you are, having some sense of the likely fluctuations before you buy isn't the worst idea in the world.

However, there are some serious weaknesses in the beta approach, even without addressing the advisability of using historical data to gauge future risk. The most basic shortcoming of beta is that there is no guarantee whatsoever that the ups and downs of the stock in question will have anything to do with the ups and downs of the overall market. Mathematicians attempt to address this problem by restricting the application of beta to those stocks with a demonstrated market correlation.

Even when correlation is not in doubt, it is vital to note that beta considers only market risk (how much the stock goes up and down), not fundamental risk (whether the company might file Chapter 11). The unfortunate truth for beta aficionados is that lousy companies can have low betas. It is perfectly possible for a stock to drop slowly, year after year, as a company's competitive position gets whittled away to nothing. At some point you wake up to find a total disaster, even though you had the apparent benefit of a low beta and therefore limited volatility. You avoided volatility to get a good night's sleep but ended up on a bed of bamboo shoots instead.

The flip side is that great companies can and do have high betas. Suppose you put on your visionary goggles and made a list of the 10 most fundamentally solid *growth stocks* you could think of. Would you expect them to have high betas or low betas? When you think about it, the answer is obvious. These stocks will have *high betas*. Market risk exists because the market has to create it. What else is the market supposed to do when a spotless growth company comes along? The market may not be efficient, but it certainly knows enough to give such a company a high multiple, and with that high multiple will come the daily fluctuations that create a high beta. The volatility is the market's way of trying to level the playing field, injecting some risk into what would otherwise be a totally superior investment.

Risk Takes Different Forms

The reason the distinction between fundamental risk and market risk is so important is that when you hear people say how long-term investors are rewarded for assuming risk, it's *market risk* they're talking about. You tend to be rewarded over time for absorbing market fluctuations, recognizing that you don't know at any given moment whether the market is merely being fussy or whether your spotless growth company has indeed sprouted a blemish. Between 1995 and 1998, there were no fewer than six trading sessions in which Compaq shares declined by 15 percent or more. Ouch! Yet the stock rose 400 percent during that same period. In the spirit of Six Flags or Coney Island, the real danger of roller coasters occurs when you try to get off in the middle.

So a volatility-averse investor can use betas to weed out stocks that figure to exceed his or her turbulence threshold, and there's nothing wrong with that; but whether that approach addresses the issue of risk is another question altogether. That's because the stock market is actually no different than the rest of life, where risk cannot be marked with permanent ink. Airplane travel was deemed obviously riskier than any other form of transportation, and we know what happened: So much effort was spent to address those risks that the statistics actually began to swing in favor of airplanes versus cars, trains, and every other mode of transportation, even if the image of riskiness remained. Similarly, open manholes represent a more obvious risk than a thin layer of snow on the ground, but any half-decent actuary will tell you that the statistics demonstrate otherwise. And when's the last time you actually saw rocks falling in a falling-rock zone?

Though our efforts to mark risk aren't always accurate, I have nothing against conservative investors. But there's a big difference between a conservatism based on knowledge (I know what's out there, and I'm troubled by it), and a conservatism based on ignorance and fear (I know that you can't catch AIDS from toilet seats, but *just in case,* I've brought along some Boraxo). Investors have to understand that being rewarded for shouldering risks doesn't mean you should buy tons of crummy companies and hope they'll turn out the way Chrysler did. Assuming *fundamental* risks is unwise unless you've truly done your homework, which is to say that the same stock can be risky in one person's hands and safe in another's. That's why investors at all points of the risk spectrum might consider augmenting their research time and dispensing with their betas.

Role Models?

So much for our discussion of risk. It's time to bring in some role models. Bargain hunters have Benjamin Graham. Contrarians have John Templeton. Traders have George Soros. Who in the world can adventurists look up to?

I'm reluctant to name names for fear of creating a jinx. When my friend Victor Niederhoffer wrote *The Education of a Speculator* in 1997, he was riding high, but his world caved in before the year was out. (I understand he's thinking about a comeback, and I wish him well.) His experience was a replay of the attention accorded such characters as Gerry Tsai and Fred Mates in the 1960s, publicity they could have done without. You don't live atop the adventurist perch indefinitely. Call it Karl Wallenda syndrome.

Among modern portfolio managers, Ken Heebner probably has the best record of any true adventurist. As the manager of the several CGM funds, including the flagship Capital Development Fund, he has piled up some ridiculously high numbers by taking aggressive stances on just a handful of stocks, a combination fraught with peril in anyone else's hands. He was an early investor in Countrywide Credit during the mortgage-origination boom; he bought shares of Bombay Company in the early 1990s and unloaded them well before the fall. Most memorably, he participated in the initial public offering of Home Shopping Network in 1986, held on despite widespread skepticism, then sold just as the historic bubble was being pierced. His Home Shopping dabbling combined the vision of a long-term investor with the vigilance of a trader, and the results were spectacular. His fund was up *99 percent* that year.

Heebner's modus operandi has been to seek out companies for which he expects earnings growth to explode—even if that growth is not sustainable for the longer term. He knows that he'll have to sell one day, but fortunately, he doesn't have too many sentimental bones in his body, so he hasn't gotten caught holding these companies after they peaked. All three of the companies just mentioned went on to have significant to devastating declines.

But one Heebner episode underscores just how important *style* is in the investment world. Believe it or not, one of his 1986 fundholders had the temerity to point out that he could have done even better that year had he simply held on to the stocks he owned in January.

Arithmetically, this was apparently true, as there was a theoretical gain of 110+ percent to be had, better than his measly 99 percent. But to view this as a missed opportunity is not only greedy, it completely misgauges what makes an adventurist tick. Just who is this person who loads up on these aggressive stocks and then sits there all year doing nothing? By now we should know enough about personalities to be able to take the bad with the good, especially when the good is giving you a 99 percent return.

GAME PLAN

Is our game plan simply to be like Ken? If so, you should know that he had to suffer through a very rough 1994, when the enthusiasm he placed in homebuilding stocks boomeranged in the face of a series of interest-rate hikes. In the wake of a double-digit loss that year, he toned down his act but managed to rebound strongly via the likes of IBM and Hewlett-Packard, proving that you don't always have to traffic in unknown names to uncover strong near-term growth. The next few years were impressive years for Heebner, but he then struggled through an extremely difficult 1998—a summer of volatile markets created double-digit losses for his funds, pretty much across the board. So now we know that you can't even think about becoming an adventurist unless you have the iron will to back it up.

Let me leave you with one final Heebner story to underscore that point. It occurred after a business luncheon in Boston at which all attendees were given extensive literature from the sponsoring company. An analyst at a rival firm noted that Heebner's eyes were glued to the literature as he walked back to his office. Too bad he didn't notice the brick wall in front of him. He walked right into it.

So if adventurism is your style, be prepared for some tough knocks. Diversify like crazy, and be prepared to relinquish in May the strong opinions you held in April. If it was easy, I'd have told you so.

Personality Spotlight

Self-Destructiveness

We made reference to self-destructive behavior in both the personality quiz and in the text. I want to make it clear that this chapter was not about curing the compulsive gambler because it's extremely difficult to give investment advice to someone with a disorder whose main side effect is to reject investment advice.

One step an over-the-top adventurist can take is to limit those funds that are subject to adventurist tendencies. The idea is to provide an outlet for all of those tendencies without risking one's entire net worth. This is just a logical extension of the principle that applies to *all* investors, which is that stock market investments should be kept apart from household funds, money for upcoming school tuitions, and anything else that cannot be jeopardized. The money to be allotted to stocks is risk capital, after all, and gets its name for a good reason.

This simple step of sequestering funds isn't always easy for the adventurist because of the brutal irony that if the funds that are being risked aren't substantial enough, some of the adventure goes away. At the extreme, we've all heard scary stories of addicted gamblers raiding their children's piggy banks. Those cases fall outside what we can reasonably hope to address in this book.

However, there are many adventurous types who can take a moment to rationally analyze the types of risks they are taking. If you are in the process of squandering the family fortune, ask yourself whether you would invest the same way with your own hard-earned money. Consider giving away some of that inherited money to a charity or cause of your choice, thereby simultaneously becoming an admired philanthropist and satisfying the selfish goal of identifying your own money issues. You just might find that your investment style changes considerably when you have a smaller sum to work with, a vital metamorphosis that few attain.

The first key word here is *guilt*, which happens to be a terrible attribute for an investor. If you feel guilty about what you've got, you will tend to be sloppy in shepherding your own money. You also won't be able to relate to the money-making pursuits of those companies in which you're investing or to the noodgy bean-counting reports of the analysts who are studying them. They'll all look greedy to you!

Which brings me to the second key word *greed*, which is in some sense the opposite of guilt. But as investment psychologist John Schott has written, greed isn't always such a bad thing, assuming that it is properly recognized and harnessed. We have always suspected that self-destructive behavior can come from those who are incredibly greedy, and now we know that it can come from those who are devoid of greed because they feel guilty. Finding a happy medium is definitely worth your while.

INCLUDE
POSTAL
ZONE NUMBERS
IN YOUR ADDRESS
ON
TAX
RETURNS

"Well, why _didn't_ you earn as much as you estimated?"

THE PSYCHOLOGY
OF ANALYZING
STOCKS

Through all of the strengths and foibles exhibited by our seven personality types, we have seen that each group is naturally associated with specific categories of stocks, as follows:

Bargain hunters–Value investments

Visionaries–Growth stocks

Contrarians–Turnarounds

Sentimentalists–Enduring franchises

Skeptics–Short sales

Traders–Short-term opportunities

Adventurists–Speculations

These correspondences are not perfect and they certainly are not one-to-one. The idea behind creating personality-based strategies is not to pigeonhole investors for their entire stock market lives. Rather, the importance of identifying groups of stocks for what they are is that the mixing and mismatching of different categories and strategies can be so destructive. Short-sellers with long time horizons can drown in margin calls; penny-pinching visionaries never get started; speculating sentimentalists get caught holding the wrong stuff.

As different as these groups of stocks are, there are simply some things with which *everyone* should be familiar as they begin their quest for stock market riches. The purpose of this chapter is to present some basic quantitative and qualitative issues of the marketplace, each discussed from a psychological point of view instead of merely from a procedural one.

QUANTITATIVE ISSUES

Price/earnings ratios. Book value. Stock splits. Random walk. That's what's in store in this section. I recognize that the intrusion of arithmetic into the stock market game isn't always welcome. The bad news is that if you aren't familiar with a few simple arithmetic tools, the market will always be an uphill battle. If you don't wish to make the effort to learn these tools, that's perfectly okay; but I only recommend this strategy for the terminally mathematically inept, who won't be able to calculate how poorly they're doing.

Seriously, though, bear with me as I review a few numerical concepts, because they aren't nearly as onerous as you might think. And if the heading "Quantitative Issues" still troubles you, remember that there is a "Qualitative Issues" section right after this one.

P/Es and Timing

We discussed price/earnings ratios at the very beginning of the bargain hunter chapter, but it doesn't hurt to review the definition. A price/earnings ratio (P/E) is just what it sounds like: the *price* of a company's stock divided by its *earnings* per share, where earnings per share (EPS) are net earnings (after tax) divided by the number of common shares outstanding. If a company is earning $2.20 per share and its stock trades at $44, its P/E is 44/2.2, or 20. The faster a company is growing, the higher you'd expect its P/E to be. Getting growth at a reasonable price is a constant challenge for all investors.

The definition of P/E may sound reasonable enough, but inquisitive types will probably note the murkiness surrounding the EPS figure. Does it refer to last year's earnings? This year's? Next year's expected earnings? Well, suppose for the sake of argument that the company in question earned $1.84 per share last year, but that it expects to earn $2.20 this year and $2.64 the year after that (roughly 20 percent growth). Take a look at the implications for the P/E:

Price/Earnings Ratios for a $44 Stock

	Earnings	Price/Earnings Ratio
Trailing	1.84	24
Current	2.20	20
Expected	2.64	16.6

Same company, same earnings trail, but a sizable change in P/E, depending on which year you're looking at. In other words, the choice matters.

The P/E Paradox

In the context of personalities, the existence of a choice of P/Es is important because some personality types accidentally "double count" in a way that exaggerates their positions. For example, the skeptic will look at the P/E table and see a stock with a P/E of 24. The logic is that even "current" earnings have yet to be achieved; they are estimates made by securities analysts, possibly with the company's guidance. It is not unusual for a company to fail to live up to these estimates, whereupon the stock market gets every bit as outraged as the accountant in the cartoon.

The skeptic is all too aware of this possibility and therefore limits the acceptable earnings horizon. The paradox is that whereas skeptics or even bargain hunters might find a P/E of 17 acceptable, they are often unwilling to look far enough ahead to make that valuation possible.

However, those who are willing to look into the future—a group that includes our friends the visionaries—will indeed see a stock with a P/E of just under 17. Depending on the circumstances, this valuation could be extremely cheap. And it will certainly be cheap as long as the company delivers on its 20 percent growth rate. However, the flip side of this position constitutes a warning to the visionary: If you look five years into the future and still can't come up with an acceptable P/E, maybe it's time to admit that the stock is fully priced after all.

News That's Fit to Print

There is one final category of P/Es that every investor should know about—the intrayear, or "newspaper," P/E. I bring newspapers into the picture because as we saw in the bargain hunter chapter, many of today's financial publications have a P/E column in their stock pages. The P/Es in question are of course trailing P/Es—newspapers don't have a staff of analysts making earnings estimates for ten thousand–plus public companies. But if you're reading the paper in September, you can be confident that the earnings are more current than those of the prior calendar year. Typically, the earnings databases give you *the most recent four quarters* worth of earnings. The implication, at least for a company whose earnings are steadily rising, is that the intrayear earnings will fall between those of the prior calendar year and the upcoming one, as will the P/E.

Beyond this timing issue, the widespread availability of newspaper data underscores perhaps the most important caveat regarding P/Es: If you don't know what's in the earnings, you shouldn't take the P/E at face value. For example, if a company takes a one-time write-off, earnings will look worse than they really are, resulting in P/Es that are either astronomical or undefined. That's what happened when Compaq purchased Digital in 1998: one day Compaq had a P/E of about 35; the next day the P/E had vanished entirely because the acquisition of Digital necessitated taking a charge that completely wiped out that year's reported earnings, even though *operating* earnings were still positive. On the other hand, if a company makes a substantial asset sale and has just booked the profit, its reported earnings will include a one-time blip that could make the P/E misleadingly low.

The moral of this section is that you should never throw around P/E figures unless you're absolutely certain what they're referring to. We would *all* do well to show a little skepticism in this area.

Book Value

I don't have much to say about book value. However, I do think that investors should understand the concept well enough to feel comfortable disregarding it.

You may be familiar with something called *shareholder's equity,* which is defined as a company's total assets minus its total liabilities. The *book value* of the company is simply the shareholder's equity divided by the number of shares outstanding.

The problem with book value is the term itself. It sounds as though there's a book someplace with the stock's true value written in it, sort of like the Blue Book used by auto dealers to tell you how much they're going to pay for your 1988 Toyota Camry. The book value feels both absolute and achievable. So when an uninitiated bargain hunter hears of a stock with a book value of $9 trading at just $6, the reaction goes something like this: "The company may be going through some tough times, but all the stock has to do is return to book value and I'm up 50 percent!"

Unfortunately, there is no Blue Book for the stock market and no guarantee that a stock trading at a discount to book value will ever make up the difference. A more likely scenario is that the company in question keeps losing money, and eventually takes a write-off that sends its book value plummeting to something like $3 per share. Meanwhile, the stock might drop to $3 a share as well. So there you are with the stock trading at book value, just as you had hoped, but you've got a 50 percent loss to show for your efforts instead of a 50 percent gain.

There may have been a time when book values were useful in approximating the value of a company in a buyout, but that time is long gone. For example, when acquisitions of brand-name companies became the vogue in the mid-1980s, most took place at several times book value, for the simple reason that the brand in question was an asset whose value could not be adequately reflected on the acquired company's balance sheet. And when the leveraged buyout era gave way to the more strategic-oriented acquisitions of the 1990s, thereagain the value of the acquired company was a function of its business fit with the acquiror, not some internal number such as book value.

Although book values are mercifully *not* provided in the daily paper, suffice it to say to that most healthy companies trade at sizable multiples of book value. For example, a P/E of 25 and a return on shareholder's equity of 20 percent correspond to a price-to-book ratio of about 5-to-1. I could bore you with all of the relationships between book value, return on equity, price/earnings ratios, and price/book ratios. But the most important warning I can give is that because book value is so readily calculated and because it sounds so important, it shows up more often than it should: lists of the 10 stocks with the lowest P/Es, the biggest discounts to book value, and so on. Bargain hunters of the world, please do yourself a favor and take these discounts with a full shaker of salt.

Stock Splits

I once made a crossword puzzle in which I clued the entry "stock split" with the definition "Sharecropper's accomplishment." If I hadn't been trying for a play on words, I might have used the following clue: "The most needlessly misunderstood phenomenon in the entire stock market." Even more than book value, stock splits represent fool's gold for the bargain hunter.

We've all heard of stock splits, but let's introduce some numbers to find out more about them. Suppose a company's stock trades at $90, and suppose that there are 20 million shares outstanding. Because the share price is relatively high in absolute terms, a potential turnoff for individual investors, the company's board may decide to split the stock 2-for-1, after which it will have 40 million shares worth $45 apiece. Note that in theory, the stock's total capitalization (share price multiplied by the number of shares outstanding) is the same. In this case, it is $1.8 billion—$90 times 20 million or $45 times 40 million.

There is nothing wrong with what the board did. What's wrong is when you hear investors saying things such as, "I want to hold on until the next split," or even worse, "I sold, and then you know what happened? The stock split two-for-one! Woe is me!"

Contrary to popular belief, stock splits do not result in immediate wealth, certainly not on the order of a 100 percent overnight gain. But the illusion of immediate wealth persists because stocks in fact often do behave well in and around the time of a split. That's because whereas splits *in isolation* are neutral events, they are seldom announced in isolation. The company's management usually announces a split when it has some other positive announcement to make, notably a favorable quarterly earnings report. You almost never hear of splits when a company's share price is tanking or when the hourly workers are on strike.

I should add that the basic logic of stock splits—to bring share prices down in absolute terms—isn't without some merit and by itself can give the stock an extra push. The lower price often attracts new investors, either because they are naive or because they can now purchase a block of 100 shares instead of settling for an odd lot of 50 shares, where commissions are typically higher. These "odd lotters," a.k.a. America's small investors, are precisely the group that the company's board had in mind. But again, you do not double your money overnight.

A final remark concerning stock splits applies to those nontraders out there who check into the market infrequently. If your heart sinks upon seeing a low share price where there used to be a high one, check for a little "s" next to the company name. That's the standard notation for a split within the prior 12 months. But don't take for granted that it is a 2-for-1 split. Many companies prefer to issue 3-for-2 splits, which are similar except for the obvious point that they don't create as big a price difference, meaning you might not be as rich as you thought. On the brighter side, there are also such things as 3-for-1 splits and 4-for-1 splits. The sky's the limit, and your friendly neighborhood broker or web site will be happy to tell you what actually came your way.

Random Walk

Have you ever wondered what the expression *random walk* actually means? In the investment world, the term was popularized by Burton Malkiel's phenomenally long-lived best seller *A Random Walk down Wall Street*. Malkiel's central thesis was that there is no stock market strategy that will outperform a simple buy-and-hold strategy over the long term. Trying to predict market dips and turns is an exercise in futility because the market's near-term behavior is essentially random. Traders beware—you are wasting your time.

But wouldn't you know that a term like random walk can get badly confused, even by financial professionals. A few years ago, toward the end of my tenure with *Worth* magazine, I joined a few of the magazine's editors in a media training session, the idea being that we wouldn't make idiots of ourselves when appearing on the *Today Show, Good Morning America*, or, more likely, a 5:30 A.M. market-watch segment on CNN. Anyway, as the media coach worked to elicit commentary from this group, someone pointed out that the market is as likely to go down tomorrow as it is to go up—a random walk, if you will. No one seemed to disagree.

The facts speak otherwise. I later asked Louise Yamada, vice president of technical analysis at Salomon Smith Barney and author of

Market Magic: Riding the Greatest Bull Market of the Century, if she happened to know the actual empirical probability of an up day in the market. She didn't know offhand, but she said she'd be happy to put her databases to work to give me an answer. I was grateful for her enthusiasm, but as I hung up the phone, I wished I had been more specific about the proper time interval. I was concerned that a study conducted over 15 or even 20 years would encompass only the bull market cited in the title of her book, in which we'd expect a positive bias.

Not to worry. She called back a few days later to tell me she had gone back *100 years.* Dating back to May of 1896, the market had 14,659 up days and 13,200 down days, making the probability of an up day 52.6 percent, not the alleged 50 percent. Thank you, Louise.

I realize that a disparity of a measly 2.6 percentage points may sound like splitting hairs. If so, it's time to find out a bit more about what a random walk really is.

The simplest form of random walk is to imagine a man standing at an X along an infinitely long, straight line. Once every second the man takes a step, which can be either one unit to the left or one unit to the right, with equal probability. If you wish to impress your friends with mathematical jargon, you might call this setup a two-dimensional, irreducible Markov chain. In more down-to-earth terms, the natural question to ask is, "What happens to the man over time?"

The answer is actually pretty damned simple. Because the probabilities of left and right movements are equal, it turns out that the X mark is a "recurrent state" of the process, meaning that if the man continues his walk forever, he will return to the X infinitely often. This conclusion is hardly surprising: If there is no leftward or rightward bias to the man's movements, the net progress over time would be expected to be zero. As a corollary, the farther away from the X mark you are, the lower the probability that he will ever get there, that probability approaching zero as the distance increases.

But let's now change the assumption ever so slightly. Let's say that the man moves to the right with probability p—say, oh, I don't know, 52.6 percent. (The probability of a leftward move is therefore $1 - p$, or

47.4 percent.) In this revised setup, although he might well return to the X several times, the expected number of visits to any one place on the line is *finite,* not infinite. Big, big difference. And the corollary is that no matter how far away you are from the starting point, it is *certain* that the random walk will one day take the man there. Any small advantage, accrued over time, converts into a huge upward shift. If the market really were a random walk with an equal chance of an up move or a down move, the Dow Jones Industrial Average would still be at the 80 level, right where it was over 100 years ago.

Those who wish to poke holes in the foregoing argument can do so in a couple of ways. First of all, investors are human beings, with all-too-finite life spans. So even if some expert on Markov chains predicts with certainty that the Dow will one day hit 1,000,000, that doesn't mean we or any of our heirs will be around to enjoy the bounty. Second, you could certainly make the argument that the world is finite and, therefore, the stock market needn't be an *infinite* Markov chain with upside probability 0.526. Here on planet Earth, nothing lasts forever.

Perhaps the best way to satisfy all parties is to suggest that the upward bias of the stock market relates to the steady rise in corporate earnings, and that the near-term behavior of the market is indeed a type of random walk around this ever-increasing earnings trend line. This is not to say that the market doesn't have its bad times; in fact, the best up days are no match for the worst down days. Whatever you do, though, don't listen to skeptics who claim that the stock market has as much chance of falling tomorrow as it does of rising. That's simply not true.

QUALITATIVE ISSUES

Now comes the news you've been waiting for—that you don't need to take an overly quantitative approach in order to succeed in the market. There were glimpses of this principle in the chapter on visionaries, but what follows has more to do with putting on your thinking cap than it does with creating visions.

Note first that all of the numbers in the prior section referred to a company's stock or trading patterns, and only secondarily to the company itself. If my purpose was to inundate you with numbers, I would have written entire sections to build upon the following staples of corporate analysis:

Debt-equity ratio. A measure of the health of a company's balance sheet. The greater the ratio, the more leveraged the balance sheet. A ratio of 50 percent means that a company's capitalization is evenly divided between debt and equity. A ratio of zero percent means that the company doesn't have any long-term debt.

Current ratio. The ratio of a company's current assets to its current liabilities. For most companies, analysts don't feel comfortable unless the current ratio exceeds 2 to 1.

Quick ratio. A ratio that is a lot like the current ratio, except it only counts cash or cash equivalents among the current assets, excluding illiquid items such as inventory. If your quick ratio isn't at least 1 to 1, you can't meet your immediate obligations. It's that simple.

And so on, and so on. But all of these ratios are just ways of quantifying the basic issues that we know to be important from personal finance: Carrying too big a mortgage is a bad thing, and being able to pay your bills on time is a good thing. Knowing what these definitions represent is as important as their actual calculation, and I'd be lying to you if I said you could make a killing solely by knowing these basic numbers—as in, "Shares of Schering-Plough tumbled today when an amateur investor (fill in your name here) discovered that the company's quick ratio had fallen to just 0.95." Still more headlines that never made it into print.

In fact, precisely because there are so many people out there doing basic securities analysis, it often makes sense to concentrate on the macro issues and leave the fine print to somebody else. Whatever your market personality, you can work on your visionary skills by taking the *anal* out of *analysis*.

In mathematics, the word for this approach is *heuristic,* which refers to a qualitative argument for a theorem or a fact whose technical proof must rely on an assortment of abstruse nuts and bolts. For example, can you prove that if 60 people are in a room, it's almost certain that at least 2 of them share a birthday? Well, I can't give you the precise probability without a computer and a whole lot of time. But it's more important to understand *why* the low-looking number of 60 is more than adequate. Namely, if you had to put 60 apples in 365 boxes, you'd come up with all sorts of ways of doing it so that no box contained 2 apples. But you'd also come up with far, far more ways in which there were 2 or more apples in one or more boxes. That's all there is to it.* Getting the idea right and appreciating the proper orders of magnitude can be just as important as calculations that are accurate to four decimal places.

Back to the stock market. One of the greatest opportunities for qualititative reasoning took place within the computer industry. If you understood that Apple Computer's unwillingness to license its software was a business decision that would haunt the company's entire subsequent history, you were a superb analyst without even having to lift a pencil. If you understood the bonanza that licensing gave to Microsoft, that's better still.

Many investors, from diehard bargain hunters all the way to adventure-loving traders, reject such heuristic, visionary thinking and prefer to go directly to actual earnings estimates. But even if earnings estimates look more concrete when you call them up on your computer

---

* This is part of the so-called "birthday paradox," which is typically presented by noting that once a room contains as many as 23 people, the odds of a shared birthday hit 50–50. By the time you get to 60 people, that likelihood has grown to over 99 percent.

screen, they are in fact the by-product of *someone else's* qualitative thinking. Remember, an analyst begins by making a variety of educated guesses that relate to such items as the pace of a company's expansion, sustainable profit margins for existing products, or the market potential of newer products. Assumptions are being made all the time. Once all of these assumptions are in place, the earnings calculation becomes purely quantitative. But just because the resulting earnings estimate appears on the page as a fixed number doesn't mean it isn't subject to variation; the long-term character of many business decisions is almost impossible to encapsulate within a near-term earnings estimate. Knowing that a particular situation is bad can be more important than knowing *how* bad.

The Apple/Microsoft dichotomy is of course a famous one, but here are some everyday questions whose mastery will enable heuristic investors to shine.

Where Does a Company Get Its Money?

You'd be surprised how many shareholders can't answer this fundamental question.

For example, a retail enterprise that expands by building and operating new stores is fundamentally different from a company that *sells franchises* to the new facilities it builds. Franchisees bring in needed capital and create a stable, predictable revenue source in the form of service fees paid to the franchisor; company-owned stores, on the other hand, are often where the action is. At McDonald's, company-owned stores have typically represented just 15 percent of total stores, but they have accounted for 60 percent of total revenues. What we're really talking about are two entirely different companies under the same roof.

A McDonald's shareholder may not have suffered by remaining oblivious to the nuances of franchising, but Boston Chicken shareholders weren't as lucky. The company created massive investor confusion by shifting between a franchising strategy and a buyback strategy. Along the way it booked dubious revenue in the form of "area development fees" from franchisors. Even if this weren't enough, a heuristic investor could also have seen as of 1996 that Boston Chicken was departing from the original concept of high-quality take-out meals and instead was making a questionable foray into the sit-down restaurant business. A name change to "Boston Market" added still more confusion. Even without knowing the precise implications of all of these maneuvers on the company's earnings, you could have sensed that something lousy was afoot. The stock fell from $40 per share in 1996 to under $1 per share in 1998. Sorry, no stock splits this time.

Is the Idea "Big" Enough?

Speaking of New England exports, Filene's Basement was another company whose once overstated prospects could have been reasoned out. The company's flagship Boston store, actually located in the basement of Filene's department store in downtown Boston, was and is something of a cult. It offers discounted merchandise year-round and made its name through its renowned seasonal sales, in which Filene's Basement would buy out the leftovers of the area's top clothing stores and offer that same apparel at sharp discounts

Despite this local success, when the company tried to clone the concept and take Filene's Basement national, it hit one roadblock after another. But couldn't this have been anticipated? For starters, the average Filene's Basement outlet wasn't a basement at all, nor did it have the Filene's store as an anchor. The entire name was a non sequitur. Furthermore, the business of close-out apparel wasn't really a national business, because there could be no guarantee that the best-selling items could be obtained on the desired scale. (It's the same principle that prevents McDonald's from selling a year-round lobster roll throughout the world.) The cloning of the original Filene's Basement was just not possible, and if you avoided the stock based on this qualitative reasoning, you were giving skepticism a good name. The stock was at $30 per share in 1993. By 1998 it had fallen to just $1 and change.

Is the Company Protected against Risks?

No company is absolutely safe from competitive risks, but some do a better job than others at dealing with them. Even for seemingly complex arenas, the underlying fundamental risks can be astonishingly simple, enabling even the most nonmathematical skeptic to move to the head of the class.

A great example of this was the savings and loan (S&L) crisis—or crises, as the case may be. Going back to the early 1980s, S&Ls were vulnerable in a way that today seems inconceivably naive. Their basic business was to invest depositors' money in long-term, fixed-income securities while paying those same depositors the prevailing short-term interest rate. But what would happen if the prevailing short-term rates spiked upward? Oops. No one bothered to ask. The answer is that S&Ls would have to pay out more than they were bringing in, and that's precisely what happened, resulting in massive losses. Beneath the complicated language of spreads, inverted yield curves, and the rest, the entire S&L crisis boiled down to a simple, flawed interest-rate model that no one had ever questioned, in much the same way that mainframe computer manufacturers never worried about the year 2000.

Having rightly discredited the old S&Ls, a skeptic had to be aware that the next generation of financial institutions might operate quite differently: From discreditation can spring redemption, provided you give it enough time, and it is vital not to let a phrase like "S&Ls are bad" become an implanted idea. Some investors still avoid REITs (real estate investment trusts) because of their crash in the mid-1970s, even though the industry has long since recoiled from the type of Ponzi scheme that made that crash possible. S&Ls had a similar cloud over them, but underneath it all they had an enormous incentive to improve.

A skeptic who is adept at identifying a company's operating risks can truly shine by switching gears and identifying those companies that insulate themselves from those same risks. (People who hated ironing were the first to embrace wrinkle-free shirts, but investors are often too spooked to notice when a wayward industry has cleaned up its act.)

Once you understood what the S&Ls went through, you'd have been in a better position to understand not only the reforms in that industry but also the tremendous efforts of mortgage agencies Fannie Mae and Freddie Mac to protect themselves and their income statements from swings in interest rates. You didn't need to know the ins and outs of variable-rate securities or duration matching. All you needed to know was that both companies figured out how to create a consistently positive spread between the rates they took in and the rates they paid out, and that's where a trained skeptic has the goods to become optimistic about the future. Both Fannie Mae and Freddie Mac retain a perception of interest-rate risk that has kept their valuations chronically on the low side; but earnings ultimately win out, and their track records since the turbulent early 1980s have been extraordinary.

How Do You Go Too Far?

Heuristic analysts have something in common with everyone else. They aren't always right.

One routine mistake made by concept-based investors (otherwise known as "faux visionaries") is investing in a company as an overly indirect "play" on a particular social or economic trend. Some of these plays are legitimate, such as the trend toward rugged outerwear that launched Timberland or the trend toward cutting health care costs that gave HMOs their years in the sun. But please don't invest in a vaguery such as an "aging baby-boomer play" unless you can trace how the favorable trend is going to boost the company's earnings column. All too often there is a huge gap between the trend (which may be legitimate) and the company's ability to ride it. It's okay to begin your investment search with a theme of this type, but it's seldom okay to end the search there.

And remember that when combing the investment universe as a qualitative thinker, it is all too easy to conclude that a stock is washed up based on a specific factor that turns out not to be the decisive one.

For example, it was easy to shy away from Coca-Cola in the mid-1990s, and you could even have sounded smart trying: Raw materials costs were higher; the dollar was stronger, which was a negative for any company with a strong international presence; the stock traded at a huge premium to the market; and so on. What more do you need to stay away from a stock? However, these notions turned out to be implanted ideas that overlooked Coke's ability to control expenses and thereby to manage its earnings quite effectively, even when several macro issues were temporarily pointing the wrong way.

In a similar vein, the major television networks suffered years of market share losses to cable TV, and the unrelenting nature of that trend made it easy to count the networks out. However, patient shareholders got the last laugh in 1995, when CBS and ABC (Cap Cities) were taken over by Westinghouse and Disney, respectively. Was this a lucky bailout? Perhaps. But a network was uniquely valuable to Disney, for example, because it could serve as an outlet for programming developed at the Disney studios. That common-sense link turned out to be the crucial component of the investment equation.

So don't be surprised as a qualitative investor when the market doesn't seem to share your concerns. Just double-check and make sure that you're looking at the right areas. If you are, you'll never have to apologize for placing number-crunching second on your list.

THE ROLE OF GAMES

It's finally time for the most qualitative approach of all. This book's title, as you may have noticed, is *The Inner Game of Investing*. The choice was not accidental because the stock market is ultimately a competition. Even if we don't have an archrival on the exchange floor, we as investors are in constant competition with the market averages. We are also in competition with ourselves, to do the best job we possibly can.

I realize that there are party poopers who view money as too serious a subject to treat as a game, but keep in mind that this book was written by someone to whom the phrase "it's only a game" never made very much sense. *Only?* Please. You can play for fun, but you compete to win. And once you recognize the competitive nature of the stock market experience, you'll see that many strategies and mindsets from the world of sports and games transfer extremely well to the investment arena.

Basketball and Volatility

There is little question that the ability to endure volatility is the hallmark of the great long-term investor. For those who aren't quite there yet, it might pay to realize that the ups and downs of many sporting contests provide great examples of volatility at work. Basketball comes the closest to mimicking the stock market because of the frequency with which the score changes and the way in which small, incremental moves can add up to huge swings. Some years ago I tested this mimicry by traipsing over to the old Boston Garden and picking up an official basket-by-basket log of a memorable Christmas Day game between the Celtics and the Knicks. I plotted the ups and downs of the game on my medieval Radio Shack pen plotter and then compared the resulting graph with a book of stock charts I just happened to have around. After a bit of searching, I came up with a company called Gerber Scientific, whose 12-year, roller-coaster stock-price history was a perfect match for the Knick-Celtics contest.

This exercise wasn't *entirely* for kicks because there's a message involved. If you're a veteran basketball fan, you know volatility as well as anyone and perhaps better than the average investor. When the better team (preferably yours) is down 15 points, you may wonder what's wrong, but you certainly don't give up hope. The players and coaches aren't panicking, so why should you? The all-important investing analogue—don't bail out of a company you believe in just because of near-term market turbulence—somehow seems more vivid with that parallel in mind; great

Knicks 113—Celtics 104

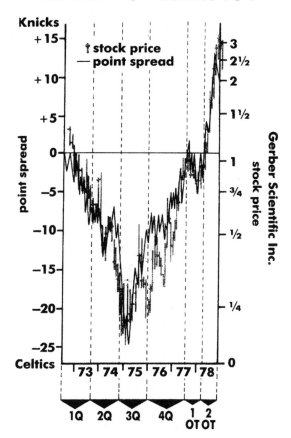

Chart courtesy of Securities Research Co. Reprinted with permission.

coaches watch the field of play, not the scoreboard. Unfortunately, the more gripped you are to the market's daily ebbs and flows, the more elusive this piece of advice will be.

Baseball and Excessive Valuations

Now for a comparison that dates back to 1984, the year my beloved Detroit Tigers started off the season with a 35–5 mark. That's right, 35 and 5. You sometimes see records like that in basketball, but never, ever in baseball. There was simply no way that the Tigers could continue to play at that pace, and therein lies a different sort of stock market parallel.

When a company's valuation seems way out of line to you, you have every right to act on that observation, either by getting rid of the stock or even by selling it short. Sometimes you just *know* that the trend can't continue, and that's how it was with the Tigers in 1984.

However, as we saw in the skeptics chapter, you are well-advised to restrict your short sales to *bad* companies that somehow garner high valuations. What you're looking for is a *decline* in the share price, not just a slowdown in upward momentum. As for the 1984 Tigers, they finished the season at 104–58 and went on to win the World Series. They were a first-rate team. It's true that following their torrid start, they cooled down to a more down-to-earth 69–53, but there's a warning here for adventurists, traders, and even skeptics: You don't make money by shorting something that's still going up.

A different type of excess arose in 1998 when Mark McGwire and Sammy Sosa blasted through Roger Maris's 37-year-old record of 61 home runs in a season. This time my message is directed at the sentimentalist, because wouldn't you know that some of the people who didn't want McGwire to break Maris's record were the same people who didn't want Maris to break Ruth's record back in 1961!

In one respect, these fans were being quite consistent: They hated the idea of change. But the attitudes toward one Roger Maris were jarringly inconsistent, which goes to show that it can be very difficult to anticipate your future sentimentality. Too bad, because this anticipation (Tom Lehrer called it "prenostalgia") could place you a generation ahead in your investment choices. You'd find yourself embracing Barnes & Noble well before there was an Amazon.com, rather than still hating them for what they did to your local bookstore. In that way you can sidestep the sentimentalist trap of aligning yourself with the old order just before it gets displaced.

Bridge—The Best Match of All?

Where investing analogues are concerned, the best game to look at may be bridge, because bridge is a mental game. Its lessons can be extremely valuable to the investor, even one who doesn't know the difference between a trump and a finesse. The late Malcolm Forbes claimed that bridge was more interesting than making money, and Warren Buffett (in *Forbes*, no less) claimed that bridge was more difficult as well. As an avid player myself,* I thought I'd build on their observations by asking you to consider the following five statements:

1. In the short term, a beginner can do every bit as well as a professional.

2. There is no single style that leads to success.

3. It is easy to outsmart yourself.

4. You can get surprisingly far simply by mastering the basics.

5. Many similar looking situations are in reality quite different.

Now look at the list again. I was talking about bridge, but are there any attributes that don't apply equally well to the stock market? Let's look at them in more detail.

1. I'm tempting fate with this analogy because it may confirm to some skeptics that investing is a game of luck. All I can say is that *of course* there is luck involved—but not nearly as much as you might think.† In rubber bridge (the kind your grandparents used to play), a

---

* In my bio on the jacket of this book, I am introduced as a life master in bridge. There wasn't room to mention that there are about five different classifications above life master, each based on the total number of "masterpoints" a player has accumulated. The highest level has about 30 times as many masterpoints as I do. Please don't tell anyone about this.

† The luckiest investment story I ever heard came from the great Pakistani player Zia Mahmood. In his book, *Bridge My Way*, he mentions that Jack Dreyfus, later of mutual fund fame, invested heavily in Polaroid in the 1950s because he thought that 3-D movies were going to take over the world. That didn't quite happen, but Polaroid introduced an instant camera instead. The rest is history.

beginner can beat a world champion with the right cards, at least for a few hands. But the *short-term* proviso is essential because a novice can't walk into high-level tournament play and emerge unscathed. If luck were everything, then a great strategy would be to bid with reckless adventurism, thereby reaching contracts that no one in his right mind would bid, and then to depend on a favorable lie of the cards to bring you home. But if it doesn't make sense to treat your card games that way, it surely doesn't make sense to take that approach with your investments.

2. This point isn't all that well understood outside of bridge, but suffice it to say that there are aggressive players and there are conservative players, as well as a wide variety of bidding systems. In tournament bridge, a spectator might know in advance when a particular hand is going to cause trouble for a specific style. What makes the stock market even trickier is that you don't have that type of certainty, but you do know that any given style won't always work. The idea is to maintain a winning style despite periodic bumps.

3. and 4. These two are intimately related. If there weren't so many people outsmarting themselves, you could never excel merely by mastering the basics.

5. This one may be the most important of all. The reason experience is deemed valuable in the stock market is that an experienced investor has the ability to recognize patterns that would surely elude the novice. This same principle surely applies to bridge. When inexperienced players get a promising but flawed hand, they tend to disregard those flaws and bid it aggressively anyway on the grounds that exciting hands don't come around very often. More-experienced bridge players take those flaws seriously, and they are aided by knowing that there's another hand right around the corner. *That* is experience working in the best possible way.

However, past experience can also create psychological dangers that beset many investors, and those dangers can be even better understood by analogy with bridge. For example, if you've just bid a small slam (hoping that your side can win 12 of the 13 available tricks) and gone down (as in failed), that negative experience might chasten you into being more conservative the next time you and your partner are dealt hands with similar potential. It's no different than shying away from a promising Silicon Valley start-up because your most recent technology investment failed. It's human. But when you think about it objectively, the statistical correlation between different bridge hands is *zero*, and investing is not much different. There is a fine line between experience and baggage, and the key is to learn from your mistakes without becoming psychologically weakened by them.

Perhaps the final analogy between games and investing is the addictive element. It's there in bridge, it's there in golf, and it's certainly there in the stock market. However well you do over a particular round or a particular year, you almost always feel you could have done better. It's that search for the eternally elusive perfection that keeps us coming back. My hope is that by drawing upon your experience as a gamesperson, you can find ways to identify stock market mistakes before they occur. Maybe, just maybe, perfection won't be quite as elusive after all.

"Oh, I'm really sorry. I just placed three million with
some broker who called five minutes ago."

DEALING
WITH
OTHERS

This chapter is somewhat multifaceted because it offers a psychological view of some longstanding fixtures of the stock market world, from professional portfolio management to investment clubs. What links these various fixtures is that they all test the ability of investors to deal with other investors, hence the title.

Until now, we have dealt almost exclusively with the challenges faced by the individual investor. As soon as you introduce someone else into the equation, anyone else, the issue of *blame transfer* arises. Consider the following conversation between a professional portfolio manager and a client. The setting is that the client has just found out about a hot new stock, and he excitedly calls the portfolio manager to get an opinion. Here goes:

CLIENT: I'm calling to get your opinion on Plasma-Lube Corporation.

MANAGER: *(Our research department doesn't cover this one. I'm sure it's gonna be a lot more trouble than it's worth.)* Plasma-Lube? I don't know. It looks awfully risky to me. Not much of a track record, you know.

CLIENT: *(Feeling a trifle put down.)* Gee, that's too bad. I thought their story looked real interesting.

MANAGER: *(Damn. The last time I said no to somebody on a speculation like this one, the stock went up fourfold and the client hasn't shut up about it. I'll try looking at the bright side.)* Well, I just pulled some information up on my computer screen. The company's earnings aren't great, but they went from three cents per share last year to five cents per share this year. Maybe they're on to something. *(Oh, brother.)*

CLIENT: *(Delighted to hear something positive.)* Great. Why don't we buy 1,000 shares?

MANAGER: *(Hey it's his money.)* Fine.

CLIENT: *(At least I got my manager's approval before buying shares on my own.)* So long. Speak to you soon.

MANAGER: *(If it goes down, I can at least say it wasn't my idea.)* So long.

The poor manager, by not objecting vigorously, unwittingly became part of the ratifying process, at least in the client's eye. Both parties can safely blame the other if something goes wrong, and in this case, something probably will. The conversation may be an exaggeration, and it is certainly fictitious, but it underscores the surprisingly poorly understood point that two people can collude to buy a stock that neither one would have bought alone.

THE WORLD OF PROFESSIONAL PORTFOLIO MANAGEMENT

The preceding example might be considered good news for those who don't have enough assets to lure a personal portfolio manager. The "good news" is sour grapes, of course, but maybe it's true that money managers aren't what they're cracked up to be.

This book doesn't take that particular view. I know many people in the business of managing money for individuals. Some of them are mediocre; some are outstanding. In short, investment management is like anything else. Yet there are some specific warning flags that you might want to factor in to a decision to hire a manger. If you haven't amassed your fortune yet, you might still benefit by knowing a bit more about the lay of the land.

Investment Experience and Mountain Rivera Syndrome

Mountain Rivera is actually a person, or at least a person's name. When Anthony Quinn delivered his magnificent performance in *Requiem for a Heavyweight,* Rivera was the name of his character. He was an over-the-hill boxer who had been beaten silly by Cassius Clay and was trying to figure out what to do with the rest of his life. Unfortunately, he didn't have the full benefit of his mental faculties. "I've been hit too many times," he lamented. And so have many professional portfolio managers.

Experience is the most-unrecognized double-edged sword in the investment business. I have never, ever seen experience described in anything but positive terms, whether it be in brochures, in television ads, or on the company letterhead. "Over 150 years of combined investment experience ..." What they're not mentioning is the potential psychological fallout we touched on in the "role of games" section: Not all portfolio managers are able to deal with the effects of repeatedly getting hit in the head—in the form of intraday "hits" to the portfolio.

If you've ever invested in the market before, you know what it feels like to see a prime holding show up in the newspaper's list of the 10 biggest decliners for the previous day. Well, magnify that experience 1,000-fold and you might sympathize with what a personal portfolio manager goes through. After all, you can put the newspaper down and continue with your life. The portfolio manager might have to field 8 or 10 phone calls from clients wondering what's going on with the stock in question. And if those calls come too early, before enough information is available to form an investment response, those 8 or 10 calls have become 16 or 20. Put enough of these episodes together, and it is only natural that many managers will get gun-shy. If you've ever felt that these money managers are overpaid, you may be right. But now you know what they're being compensated for. It's not necessarily for their stock-picking genius. They're being paid to absorb the daily vicissitudes of the market, for which they often pay a big price.

Earlier in the book I mentioned having spent some time in the mid-1980s as an analyst for a small firm that specialized in individual portfolio management. One day I fielded a request from a client to look into a company called DNA Plant Technology, which was then trying to market genetically altered vegetables under the name Veggie Snax. I looked at the company and concluded that it was way too early to buy, and I communicated that conclusion to the head of the firm. His response was a textbook case of Mountain Rivera syndrome: "What if the stock goes up to 20?" (It was then at 11 or so.) Well, my analysis made me conclude that such a climb was against the odds, yet I could hardly say it was impossible—we are talking about the stock market, aren't we? But I soon realized that his response had nothing to do with such fine points as probabilities or even securities analysis. It was simply his experience that when he says no to any client-initiated stock and it takes off, he never hears the end of it.

Well, it was probably two months after that conversation that I left the firm—do you blame me?—so I never got to see the downfall of DNA Plant Technology. Nor, tragically, did the head of the firm, who committed suicide just a few years after he and I last spoke. True story, I'm afraid. I wish I could have ended this section on a more upbeat note, but perhaps it's more important to underscore the fact that Mountain Rivera syndrome can be serious if left unchecked. If you find yourself getting

beaten down by the market, you're not gaining experience, you're gaining pain. Take a break.

The Approved List and the Lack Thereof

A different but related difficulty faced by many personal portfolio managers is that the list of stocks for which they are responsible is simply
way too big. Remember, most new clients other than lottery winners
will come in already owning a bunch of disparate stocks. If each client
has one or two stocks that no other client owns, it doesn't take long before a manager's list reaches 50 stocks—50 stocks that only one person
owns, any one of which can be the subject of an overnight implosion
and the resulting phone-call sequence.

The institutional approved list, or coverage list, is one way out of
this mess. By restricting the core holdings of clients' portfolios to an established list of companies, a firm hopes to bring a uniformity to the investment process and in so doing to relieve individual managers of a
potentially hopeless monitoring task. As long as the list doesn't exceed
a few hundred companies, the firm will be able to provide research coverage to all of these core holdings. This coverage may seem less important in the information age, but it remains the basic value-added
component of a money management firm's capabilities. Why should a
client choose them over anyone else but for the superiority of their in-
house research?

However, what most clients don't understand is that the creation of
an institutional list is by necessity a bureaucratic process that makes it
very difficult for the firm to be current. Many stocks are kept on the list
far longer than they should be, either because of analyst inertia or simply because there are so many clients who own the damn thing. I remember that precise situation arising in the early 1980s, when I was an
apprentice analyst at Scudder, Stevens and Clark. The chemicals analyst
wanted to get rid of the old Allied Chemical, in part because it was such
a nuisance to cover. An uproar ensued, with managers in New York,

Boston, Cincinnati, and who knows where else complaining that their clients had been left holding the bag.

But my favorite approved list story is a red flag to any contrarian who is contemplating hiring a portfolio manager. At the very beginning of my second calendar year at Scudder, I came upon the seemingly innocuous news that the prior year's in-house stock-picking contest had been won by someone who picked a company called Wyle Laboratories. I happened to be walking by the office of the head of equity research that day, so I thought I'd strike up a conversation. I asked him why nobody had picked Chrysler. After all, the year in question was 1982, the single biggest year in Chrysler's comeback and a year in which the stock had gained over 300 percent. The research director's reply was right to the point. "Because it's not on our list," he said. Being new to the firm and to investments in general, I had no idea what he was talking about. He went on to explain that because of the fiduciary responsibility the firm had toward its clients, it was impossible to recommend a company that was flirting with bankruptcy. That's why Chrysler had been taken off the list.

The comical part of the story is that Chrysler was quietly added *back* to the coverage list some three years later, at which point the company's return to financial health eliminated the fiduciary worry. Of course, that same financial health also eliminated the stock's appeal as a rebound candidate, but you can't have it both ways. Clients who thrived on finding such rebounds were out of luck. More generally, it pays to know whether the firm that's handling your money is of a personality compatible with yours.

Coverage lists can also be handicapped by personnel considerations in a way that the visionary would find intolerable. For example, although "emerging growth" is a generically attractive category that no investor would want to be left out of, the wide-ranging nature of the category can wreak havoc from the vantage point of a director of research. When a company comes along that is just plain *different,* whom among your stable of analysts do you call on to cover it? Does the computer analyst get assigned to cover Yahoo!, or is it the media analyst? Maybe you have to hire someone new. Maybe you can't find anybody, and the company never makes it to the list. These types of staffing decisions are invisible to the average client, but collectively they can go a long way toward influencing the performance of that client's portfolio.

One positive point about approved lists is that they at least recognize that portfolio managers are human beings and can't know everything there is to know about every single stock out there. Sometimes the public forgets this simple fact. Remember the 1970s' TV show *Medical Center,* with Chad Everett as Dr. Joe Gannon? Gannon had the title of associate professor of surgery, and he proved equally facile in operating on the brain, gall bladder, big toe, and everything else in between, never mind that his feats represented over 60 combined years of medical training.

Have you ever watched a financial expert on one of those cable TV shows where viewers phone in their own questions? Well, having been in the expert's seat on several occasions, I can tell you that callers treat you like the market's equivalent of Joe Gannon. You're supposed to know *everything.* But as a practical matter, unless the stocks are screened beforehand or unless you get lucky with the questions, the responses are a complete joke. They are inevitably steeped in generalities that have everything to do with maintaining the expert's telegenicity and very little to do with aiding the actual shareholder. The most honest response—"Sorry, but I really haven't studied that particular stock"—is a sure way to look like an idiot on national TV.

Remember, great investors like you have *styles.* Even if you hold only a few stocks, those precious holdings have come about by scanning the entire market universe for those special companies that fit your bill, whether they be value companies, growth companies, turnaround stories, or whatever. There is no way that an approved list can be flexible enough to accommodate this very natural approach. Lists are really the stock market's equivalent of an arranged marriage, with infidelity the inevitable result.

Time Is of the Essence

This point has already been made implicitly, but it's important enough to state as a general rule. The typical professional portfolio manager does not have the time in the day to be a superior investor.

This is good news of sorts for those of us who lack the financial resources to hire a portfolio manager in the first place: Perhaps we're not missing as much as we first thought—except the money, of course. But even if we have amassed the requisite minimum portfolio, we might want to think about whether we want an advisor for the sake of investment performance or for the sake of a personal relationship that is centered around money and security but that is not purely performance driven. All too often we delude ourselves into thinking we're getting both performance and a relationship, but the human factor makes that combination a prodigious task, never mind what you read in the brochures. It is virtually impossible for one person to handle the phone calls that provide the personal touch as well as the research that provides results.

The exact same principle applies to brokerage firms. If you've placed your money with a full-service broker and enjoy working with whoever handles your account, terrific. But don't expect your broker to be the Shell Answer Man. Brokers have very little time to read even their own firm's research. They are adventurists at heart, and the market's daily wanderings can consume much of their attention, if only because executing trades is the lifeblood of their business. Contrary to popular belief, most brokers aren't sleazy. Personally, I am amazed how many of them can maintain at least a cursory knowledge of hundreds of stocks. But if you're on the investment side of the street, a little knowledge can be a dangerous thing. You're better off having a thorough knowledge of 5 companies than a cursory knowledge of 500.

Ultimately, the one question you must answer is this: If you're looking for someone to help you manage your money, would you rather have them pay attention to you or to your money?

THE FINANCIAL PRESS

The pressures faced by the financial press are quite different from those faced by, say, the manager of a mutual fund. Whereas the mutual fund manager can in theory buy and sell a particular stock without the customer base ever finding out, financial journalists have to state their preferences in print, a medium that is public, visible, and final until proven otherwise.

When it comes to stock recommendations, the effects of this visibility are widespread. One noteworthy effect is the rarity of the table-pounding buy recommendations. That's because the pursuit of balanced journalism creates a pressure to tell both sides of the story, resulting in articles that are full of qualifiers and devoid of the sort of zest that says, "I own this stock and I think you should, too." In fact, journalists have to be extremely careful when they mix ownership and authorship, lest they trigger the ever-latent suspicion that the article was written in order to boost one of the author's lagging holdings.

Skeptics' Delight

When you put all of these pressures together, what happens is that leading financial journalists are skeptical to a fault. Society doesn't dole out very big penalties for misplaced skepticism, and financial journalism takes this leniency to new heights. Alan Abelson of *Barron's* was about as upbeat as a mortician while the Dow marched from 1,000 to 9,000, but no one seemed to mind. Jim Grant of *Grant's Interest Rate Observer* has been bearish for eons, but if you thought his publication would go out of business as a result, guess again. Perhaps Grant's enduring success can be traced to the eloquence with which his overly negative market commentaries have been communicated. But an even better guess is that he has found a thriving market of skeptics, all of whom are subtly buoyed by the fact that Grant's stumblings are more visible than their own.

And just think of the attention we accorded the likes of Elaine Garzarelli for calling the 1987 crash, to say nothing of Joe Granville before her or Ravi Batra afterward. By comparison, John Templeton's avuncular reassurance of bull markets ahead after 1987's Black Monday is barely remembered. The mindboggling irony is that negative forecasts get so much press because they're so much harder to make than positive ones—the market will go up over time. But if that's the reason skeptics get attention, why be one?

My former *Worth* colleague Jim Jubak was victimized by the allure of calling the big collapse in a cover story he wrote for the magazine in February 1997. The conclusion, trumpeted in bold for all to see, was that Microsoft had ceased to be a viable investment, much less an attractive one. Pages of tables and charts supported his conclusion, which was largely based on valuation. Even in the best of worlds, the article couldn't foresee anything above 11 percent annual appreciation in Microsoft stock.

Alas, the average reader of a financial magazine doesn't have any insight into the personality of the author and/or editors, and in this case those personalities proved decisive. As an insider of sorts, I knew Jim to be a first-rate investor, but it was more accurate to say that he was a brilliant investor who suffered from occasional bouts with hyperskepticism, which in turn made me skeptical about the article's conclusion. The allure of calling an end to the Microsoft reign was a powerful carrot stick—too powerful, perhaps. The persuasive tone of the article notwithstanding, Microsoft shares rose over 100 percent in the year that followed and had tripled by the time Windows98 debuted. But give Jim credit, because by then he had admitted his mistake in a most honorable way. He left his position at the magazine and went to work as an online columnist for Microsoft.

One additional reason for the paucity of table-pounding buy recommendations is that they smack of boosterism, which by definition is unprofessional. *Columnists* can be boosters at their own peril, but general articles, even bylined articles, don't have the same flexibility. Unless the byline is awfully familiar, the piece reflects on the magazine, not the individual. Keep in mind that magazines make their money via advertising, and there is a tacit wall set up between those who sell the ad space and those who create the content. It is an editor's worst nightmare to promote the stock of a company that just happened to advertise in the magazine. More commonplace is the ad salesperson's worst nightmare—a negative piece about a company that just signed up for a two-page spread. In the best of worlds, those problems will be solved prior to publication, but in any event, they are the salesperson's problems and not yours. You as a reader are still affected by this invisible process, though, because you end up reading publications that are more negatively charged than might really be necessary.

Skeptics' Revenge

One type of magazine article that you *should* be skeptical about is the type that lists the top five or so picks of some well-known money manager. The first problem is that because of space considerations, the actual descriptions of these companies can be extremely short, the apparent idea being that mere ownership by a star investor should be enough to get you interested. But halo effects are vastly overrated. If you do buy, do you really think that the same star investor is going to be there holding your hand? If you don't know why you bought, you won't know when to sell, so it is imperative that you at least understand the style of the manager in question, lest you be left holding the bag. This is especially true for managers who are traders or adventurists.

My favorite such story took place in the mid-1980s, when our friend Ken Heebner of Capital Development Fund fame was quoted in an article as being wild about Universal Furniture, a low-cost producer based somewhere in Southeast Asia and a company I knew about only because I had seen the prospectus for its then-recent public offering. Suddenly the company was in the limelight. I excitedly called the broker who had sent me the prospectus, at which point I found out to my surprise and amusement that Heebner had already sold his position. No, there was no hanky-panky here, just the perils of a publication delay.

The double twist that makes the Universal Furniture story memorable is that Heebner was wrong to sell! He had bought at the initial offering price of $11 and decided to take a profit at $18 or so, but the company was bought out at $40 per share within two years. If professionals can be wrong on the sell side, they can be wrong on the buy side, too—all the more reason to be skeptical of the halo effect. Know what you're buying.

Space for Rent

My own experience as a financial columnist brings up one final issue that the public doesn't take into account—the need to fill space. I alluded to this need in a positive sense in an earlier chapter: There are many winning stocks I uncovered solely because I had a byline to fulfill. The flip side, of course, is the pressure to find an unreasonably high number of winners. Some of the great investors of all time have made their mark via a mere handful of great stocks. They wouldn't relish the prospect of finding new ones week after week or even month after month. But if they tried to write up the same ones in every issue, their editors would have a fit.

A personal example of the perils of excessive volume requirements arose with retail stocks. Some years ago I suggested in a column that retail investors might do well to concentrate on the stocks of the big chains such as Wal-Mart, Staples, and CompUSA, *and forget everything else.* This wasn't good news for contrarians, sentimentalists, or bargain hunters, but I was just calling it as I saw it. Even though most of these stocks carried high price/earnings ratios, their earnings growth was, on balance, so powerful that the stocks couldn't help but follow suit. As for me, I should have quit while I was ahead because practically anything else I had to say about retail stocks was a giant step backward. In particular, my searches for more value-oriented retail investments (Caldor?, Woolworth?) were often well off the mark.

There is a related aspect of life as a financial writer that readers would do well to appreciate. When pitching an idea for a new story, the writer has to be aware that relevance and timeliness are always on an editor's mind—as in, "Okay, Derrick, this is a perfectly good company all right, but why *now?*" To my discredit, I have often come up short in my response.

You will note that this predicament is a variation of the "buying moment" perils we looked at in the introduction, perils that affect all investors. There are many wonderful companies that never make it into our portfolios because they had the audacity never to provide that single, magical moment that had "buy" written all over it. It wasn't until I had been a columnist for many years that it occurred to me that I could write a *column* about this very phenomenon, thereby introducing some quality blue-chip stocks that were merely attractive long-term investments, not attractive investments *now*. My editor loved the idea, and the article was well received. I only wish I had written it five years earlier.

So I guess the secret is out. Financial writers are human beings, too, and it pays to know a little something about the ones you're reading.

INVESTMENT CLUBS

So you're thinking of starting an investment club? You're already in one? You're one of the Beardstown Ladies? No matter. Wherever you happen to be in the process, you'll find that investment clubs create a unique environment for the unfolding of stock market psychology.

The most obvious difference between your own investment decisions and those of your investment club is that the club's decisions are group decisions. As such, these decisions are governed by group behavior as well as by fundamental investment merit.

To show you what I'm driving at, you may remember that I talked about the issue of flexibility in the chapter on traders. At the time, I introduced an important criterion: Would you be willing to get back into a stock you owned in the past, especially if that prior experience was unfavorable? If the answer is yes, then you can count yourself among the flexible investors of this world. But if you think about that same criterion in the context of a group, you can't help but conclude that almost all investment clubs are not only inflexible, they are more likely stiff as a board.

For example, suppose your group once got burned on Egghead, the discount software company. (The stock in fact swooned from $30 to $3 between 1992 and 1997, during which time the company was consistently unprofitable.) You decided to revisit that fiasco and discovered that the company was engineering a major turnaround. Would you suggest to the club that you get back in? Can't you hear the groans already? It is the very rare group that will be receptive to an idea like that. As a rule, the only way a group will relent is if you make your case so strongly and with such gusto that they capitulate to your iron will. But realize that in winning any such victory, you will absorb all of the blame if it goes wrong and only a small percentage of the gain if it goes right. With odds like that, it's no wonder that getting back into a stock is so uncommon for an investment club.

For the record, Egghead had changed its stripes in a very dramatic way. It scrapped its retail stores altogether in favor of conducting software auctions over the Internet (via an acquisition of a company called Sterling Software). The stock of the new egghead.com, which got as low as $3 in the summer of 1997, moved into the mid-$20s when the success of these auctions reached the company's bottom line the following summer. But your investment club could pretty much kiss that gain good-bye.

A different hazard that investment clubs would do well to avoid is getting bogged down in the same old tedious conversations.

The Setup

"Why don't we buy J. P. Morgan? It's a great company."

"Yes, it is, but the price is too high."

"Okay, let's wait for it to come down a bit. Then we can buy."

Two Months Later

"Look. J. P. Morgan is down eight points from when we first looked at it."

"Yeah. Glad we didn't buy it. Wonder what's wrong with them?"

Six Months Later

"Look. J. P. Morgan is twenty points higher than it was when we first looked at it."

"Yeah, it's twenty-eight points higher than it was six months ago."

"Should we buy some?"

"No, it looks too high to me."

Is this drivel, or what? Conversations like this are like tic-tac-toe. The first time you encounter them, they hold a certain fascination. But if you never get bored discussing absolutely generic stock-price behavior, you've got a big, big problem. So as long as we're here, let's dissect this particular conversation a bit more.

The first part—in which a stock is rejected because it is a couple of points too high—is the classic method whereby a group weasels out of a real decision. Even worse, the "argument" is straight out of *Babes in Toyland*. Finding good stocks is hard enough in the first place. Do you really expect that the one you've found is going to backtrack a few points for your benefit and *then* resume its skyward march? Maintaining a tight price discipline is one thing, but it's quite another to demand that a stock follow the trading pattern of your dreams.

The second part of the conversation reveals that the "tight price discipline" to which I just referred can be a total fallacy. Even when a stock slides back into the preferred buying range, it doesn't necessarily get bought. Either the club members get greedy, hoping for an even bigger decline, or they get worried, wondering what prompted the stock to fall in the first place. Or maybe they don't notice the decline at all because the stock was effectively in the discard pile after the prior conversation. Only *rarely* does a group actually buy a stock after a decline that drops the stock to the price at which the group said it would buy it in the first place. You follow?

However, rather than pick on group processes, perhaps we should admit that the wretched conversation we just saw is one that many of us have had with *ourselves,* albeit silently. In that sense, investment clubs can be a wonderful device, provided you can harness the group process to avoid these conversations once and for all. To reach that goal, consider appointing someone in the group as a watchdog for the generic patterns we've just discussed. Rotate the watchdog role if necessary; the only real criterion is that the person has the respect to command the attention of the group. Whoever is in that role should devise some sort of signal to tell the others, "Excuse me, our discussion has degenerated into generic pablum."

The watchdog role needn't end there. Remember, it is easy enough for investment club participants to identify the specific stock selections that went awry, but it is a taller order to sort out the *types* of mistakes that the club can blunder into. If the club has suffered opportunity costs because people always wanted to buy a few points under the prevailing price and the market didn't accommodate, that point should be noted. If the group always sells too soon, that pattern should be noted.

These patterns, like many of our personal faults, are more readily noticeable within a group format, whereas they could remain hidden for years in our personal investing psyches. With group monitoring and intervention, these patterns needn't repeat themselves.

Another countermove your club might consider is using secret ballots for all investment decisions. Demand a two-thirds majority before investment action is taken. The very existence of such a vote can provide interesting material for the watchdog. Are the stocks that get a 100 percent approval rating the ones that end up being successful? Are the ones that barely squeak by better or worse? And what about the ones that just miss out? How do they end up doing over time? Did the group get unlucky in the "ones that got away" column? Or was the group not looking in the right places to begin with? If you don't know the answers to these questions, it's going to be difficult to improve.

If you find yourself reacting with ambivalence to the watchdog concept, I should underscore that the purpose of a whistle-blowing watchdog is not to render people silent, nor is it to make the club meetings less fun. That would defeat the whole purpose of the club.

I remember an early experience with systemization, and I have to admit I didn't like it. It happened one January weekend many years ago when some friends and I were clearing the snow off a neighborhood pond in hopes of getting a hockey game going. Our approach to the challenge was utterly aimless until a couple of older kids (14-year-olds) came by to inject some discipline into the process. From that point on we shoveled in a logical, Zamboni-like progression. I wasn't too happy about the change. Whether I disliked the system or felt stupid about not having thought of it myself, I cannot say. The one result I couldn't dispute was that we were playing hockey a helluva lot sooner than if those kids hadn't shown up.

The moral is that some systemization doesn't have to spoil the fun. The watchdog's signal can be hitting a pinata with a wiffle-ball bat, if that would provide the needed levity. The idea is to improve the quality of the conversations, not to silence the group. If aimless conversations about share-price volatility are like tic-tac-toe, then perhaps it's time to move up to checkers, chess, or what-have-you. There are different levels of the game, and I'd hate for your club to get stuck at the wrong level.

With any luck, your club will avoid the worst pitfall of all for group processes—the possibility that *no one* in the group is happy with the structure of the portfolio. That possibility was a lesson I learned after my first couple of institutional investment committee meetings. I remember coming out of a meeting whose purpose was to establish guidelines policy for the firm's model fixed-income portfolio. Should it consist of 30 percent government bonds? 20 percent corporates? 15 percent mortgage-backed securities? If the percentages sound arbitrary to you, then you know how I felt. But feelings ran high. People left the room bewildered that their colleagues couldn't understand why a 10-to-15 percent range for zero-coupon bonds was far superior to a 5-to-10 percent range. That's democracy for you. Everyone gets a say, but no one likes the result. Surely your club can do better.

The subject of doing better brings us to the very last issue for your investment club: calculating investment performance. Would you believe that this calculation can be ridiculously complex? Whenever you are constantly adding money to a portfolio, the performance for that portfolio has to be broken down into bite-sized time frames, and the individual performance figures must then be spliced together to get a final figure. Note that I said "spliced together," not "added." You should not try to perform these calculations yourself, any more than you should pull the tag off your mattress. You need software to accomplish this task, and I'm told that the National Association of Investors Corporation (NAIC) is one place that might be able to point you in the right direction.

Remember, though, that you should set your expectations realistically. If the market is going up, your club's relative performance will always suffer to the extent that your portfolio contains cash, because even a fully invested portfolio won't always be able to put the cash to work immediately. But the good news is that the difficulty of performance calculation means that your group can spend its time thinking about investment ideas and not stewing over how you're doing, because sometimes you won't really know.

Then again, if you calculate your performance incorrectly, you can always write some books about your success and then sheepishly admit later that it was too difficult to sort out the exact figures. (You didn't think I'd write an entire section on investment clubs without taking friendly aim at the Beardstown Ladies, did you?)

"Tell me, Charlie—anything in those indicators of yours about a divorce?"

INVESTING
IN REAL
LIFE

The issues we'll raise in this final chapter are so basic that you may wonder why we didn't encounter them earlier. However, a lot of groundwork had to be covered before we were ready to face the real world and talk about the actual day-to-day management of your budding portfolio. Besides, ever-mindful of the different personality types out there, I realized that many folks like to read books starting from the back, and I didn't want to disappoint them. So whatever your investment personality, here are some basic questions you'll encounter in your real-life stock market journey.

HOW MANY STOCKS
SHOULD YOU OWN?

This is a devilish question that has lasted through the ages. Before giving my final attempt at an answer, let me convey the two sides of the "how many stocks" debate as neutrally as I possibly can.

You Should Own Only a Few

Some years ago, at a small New York investment house called Central National, a gentleman named Arthur Ross compiled a spectacular but largely unsung record in the stock market. His style was conservative by nature, and his portfolio was consistently devoid of the growth stocks normally associated with superior performance, all of which beckoned one visitor to ask Mr. Ross for his secrets of investment success. "Tennis shoes," Ross replied.

If Ross's success seemed inexplicable before the question, it had taken on new heights with that explanation. The shaken visitor had no choice but to ask one of Ross's colleagues what in the world his mentor had meant.

"No, you've got it all wrong," the colleague explained with a laugh. "He must have said 'ten issues,' not 'tennis shoes.' Ten stocks is the most he's ever owned."

Perhaps the most popular incentive for owning a handful of stocks is that if any one of them takes off, the portfolio will benefit disproportionately. If you own 100 stocks and one of them triples, your net holdings have gone up by all of 2 percent. But if you own just 10 stocks and one of them triples, your net has gone up by 20 percent. Better.

But Arthur Ross was thinking along a somewhat different line. His contention was that a decision to concentrate your holdings should produce an automatic constraint on the types of stocks you will be investing in. There should be no speculations and no crummy balance sheets. In short, the holdings should represent little or no *business* risk (as distinguished from market risk), if only because a single calamity would have such a devastating effect on the portfolio.

Stylewise, Ross would have to be described as a franchise investor, which has to be considered a fairly conservative category. Ken Heebner, a true adventurist, also advocates a small number of stocks, but his choices have been consistently more aggressive, which explains why the returns from his fund have often deviated so sharply from the typical fund or even the S&P. (Fortunately, these deviations have been in the right direction, if we're willing to overlook 1994 and 1998.)

Whatever your style, the restriction to a handful of stocks behooves the investor to be extremely well informed on each and every holding, *and it makes the requisite hours of research feasible.* The average investor doesn't have the time to masquerade as a miniature mutual fund.

You Should Own a Bunch

The benefits of owning a handful of stocks can become liabilities if things don't go the right way. Even the best long-term investments can move adversely for months or perhaps years, and the concentrated investor will inevitably stagnate during those times.

Owning a bunch of stocks makes sense for aggressive investors such as traders, adventurists, and even visionaries. Although a greater number of stocks dilutes the importance of any given one, that dilution may be an appropriate balance if you are already leaning toward the high risk/high return segment of the market. Furthermore, the more investment ideas you have, the more important it is that they be spread out. There is no reason to artificially restrict the number of portfolio holdings if you honestly feel strongly about 30 or even 50 stocks. And there is nothing more frustrating than creating an attractive "initial cut" of stocks, only to underperform because your final cut included the wrong ones. This type of experience is what prompted

Peter Lynch to become the poster boy for the "own a lot" set, and there is no denying its effectiveness.

Lynch's philosophy was that if you chance upon an industry you like, why in the world should you place all of your bets on one company in the industry rather than spread the wealth around? For example, a "one stock" oil investor in the 1980s could have chosen Texaco, only to see the company pushed into bankruptcy by the Pennzoil litigation while Exxon, Mobil, Chevron, and the rest were doing just fine. Strange things can happen, and you need protection. With few exceptions, the only time you really and truly must choose the single best stock in an industry is when you've picked the wrong industry.

Resolution?

Unfortunately, most new investors across all personality types decide that owning a handful of stocks is best for the simple reason that they don't have enough money. The risk here is that those investors' entire worth (and future associations with the stock market) can boil down to the performance of one or two stocks at a particular time. If those stocks succeed, the investors will have more money, with which they can diversify. If they're really lucky, they'll go on to manage a $20 billion mutual fund, at which point they'll have to own so many stocks that their performance will inevitably become mediocre. Sigh.

The more I think about it, the more I'm convinced we have it all backwards. New investors should start off by owning a bunch of stocks, even if it means owning seemingly trivial amounts in any given one. This approach wouldn't have been feasible a generation ago, but with the arrival of super discount commissions, it can be done. This spread-out portfolio allows us to get a real stock market education, as well as to develop a keen understanding of our own stock market personality. Once this double-barreled education has taken place, we can shift to a smaller number of holdings, never mind that we might have enough money to accommodate more. In this way, we'll all be placing our biggest bets at the time of our greatest knowledge and experience, rather than the other way around. Just a thought.

HOW OFTEN SHOULD YOU MONITOR YOUR STOCKS?

As with the issue of how many stocks you should own, the issue of how frequently to check up on those stocks is a highly personal matter. The two are related in the sense that the more stocks you own, the more time you must spend monitoring them. But let's again look at the issue in debate form, with each side laying out its case.

You Should Check in Every Day

Of course you should check in every trading day. As long as the market is open, a stock's price can change, and any responsible investor would want to know about that change. You open up the morning paper, and you check the holdings of greatest interest to you. That's the tradition that has been followed for the better part of a century, and it works well for many investors, traders and nontraders alike.

The emergence of online stock-price retrieval has changed that tradition for the better. Even though the prices you see online might be subject to a 15-minute delay, intraday prices are far more valuable than whatever you might see at the breakfast table. The prices you see in the newspaper tell you where the stock closed the night before, but if that same newspaper also contains bad news for the company in question, you have no assurance that you'll be able to exit at that same price. So if your daily routine includes a midday online checkup, you'll be able to take action, if action is called for. In today's age of rapidly changing information, you can't afford to be left behind.

You Should Check in Once a Month

Believe it or not, there are many serious investors who have no interest in following their stocks every day. Once a month or so is deemed adequate enough, and there are surprising benefits to this approach. The most obvious benefit is that you can truly see patterns developing in a way that can elude the everyday onlooker. It's your daffy old aunt whom you see every couple of months who notices how much your children are growing (or how much weight you're gaining), not you. In the stock market, you sometimes have to give events enough time to happen in order to develop a sharper understanding of the long-term link between corporate performance and share-price performance. (The "month" time frame is of course somewhat arbitrary. It could be two weeks or three months, depending on the individual.)

And although it's easy to think that the trader/constant market watcher will be able to bail out of a losing stock much quicker than his or her lackadaisical counterparts, the reverse can be true. How can you possibly lose 30 points on a stock that you're watching every day? Simple. One point at a time, that's how. I remember well the plaintive cry from an exasperated portfolio manager in 1984: "I bought Coleco at 16 and sold at 16. But in between it was 65!"

By contrast, the once-in-a-while investor might see the first 10-point hit in one gulp, then use that version of shock therapy to commit to a reinvestigation of the reasons why the stock was attractive in the first place. If its attraction is gone and a sale ensues, there's a 20-point advantage right there. The tortoise can beat the hare, fair and square.

Avoiding the market's daily drumbeat keeps your mind fresh, no mean feat in this age of information inundation. I remember hitting my saturation point on a long weekend drive, when I was supposedly on my own time. I took a much-needed rest stop, only to be reminded that Swisher, the manufacturer of those little red urinal screens, was a public company: It said so right on the product. Did I really need to know that? Given the setting, I feel I got my revenge, but it just goes to show how pervasive the stock market's influence has become.

There are also some more cosmic issues that you might want to think about, issues we touched on in the trader chapter: If you spend all day clicking ticker symbols, it's fair to ask whether there might be some more productive use of your time. The retirees who congregated at the neighborhood brokerage to watch the tickertape go by didn't have anything better to do, but at least the market provided an excuse for companionship and discussion. Retrieving prices online removes that social function altogether.

Just What Are You Checking?

The major flaw in the preceding discussion is that it appears to define *checking into a company,* whatever the frequency, as checking on its share price first and then taking action (or not). But I should stress that *following* a company should involve much more than mere share-price considerations. A true investor is not merely someone who reacts to stock-price changes.

Today's online news-retrieval capabilities make it easier than ever to truly follow a company from the ground up. The information is organized by ticker symbol and surely more complete than you could ever hope to cull for yourself, even with 10 newspaper and magazine subscriptions. That's where your online research time should be spent.

And remember that the frequency with which you check into a company's fundamentals is surely dependent on the nature of what you own. If you're a sentimentalist and you own shares of a blue chip like Kellogg, you really don't expect the company's basic business to change overnight. That may be why you own it in the first place. Fair enough, but if you own Micron Technology or some other company whose earnings are directly dependent on items (i.e., semiconductor prices) that you don't run across every day, then you might have to do some additional legwork to stay current.

When I say that everyone should find a pattern that suits them, I mean just that. If you're champing at the bit to find out how your stocks are doing, then assuage those feelings and punch some ticker symbols. If you punch so frequently that you realize you're obsessing instead of investing (admittedly, this may be easier for someone else to notice than for you), then you've gone too far. There's no rocket science here, perhaps not even any earth science. But every individual investor would do well to figure out the most comfortable pattern.

PUTTING IT ALL TOGETHER: THE PORTFOLIO

Throughout most of this book, our attention has been focused on individual securities, in terms of either research or potential purchase or sale. You'd think that building a portfolio would be as simple as putting a bunch of individual selections together, but it's not so.

A tennis player could have told you that portfolio construction involves a whole new dimension. Consider the following parallels between what an investor does and what a competitive tennis player does:

A tennis player . . .	A stock market investor . . .
Stage 1. Practices intensely	Researches intensely
Stage 2. Plays individual matches	Buys individual securities
Stage 3. Plays in tournaments	Builds a portfolio

The gap between stage one and stage two is obviously considerable because it amounts to the difference between a dress rehearsal and the real thing. But the gap between stage two and stage three is not as widely recognized. What tennis players come to realize is that there are intangible factors of self-confidence, determination, and focus that make winning a tournament a much bigger feat than simply winning the individual matches. And investing is much the same.

At some point in the portfolio-construction process, every individual investor makes a most unwelcome discovery: You don't always have enough money to buy everything you might want to. You are forced to ask questions along the lines of, "How much do I really like this stock?" "Don't I like this other one better?" Suddenly you find yourself making weird comparisons, as between an international airline and a Mississippi steakhouse. You sometimes end up deciding between two stocks you like equally, knowing that only the ones that actually make it into the portfolio will determine your performance.

We encountered this same finiteness-of-money problem when talking about investment clubs, and at the time I made the recommendation that someone should keep track of the stocks that never quite made it. This type of monitoring used to be totally impractical for the individual investor because the neurotic nature of the pursuit would outweigh any benefits. Fortunately, technology has made this monitoring task ridiculously easy. Online services can give you the opportunity to create as many paper portfolios as you want, including your real one. While it may be no fun to see that your make-believe electronic portfolio is outperforming your real one, it's important for new investors to identify costly decisions. Better still, it may not be too late to rectify them.

Selling within a Portfolio

The fine art of selling may be the best illustration of the difference between individual decisions and *portfolio* decisions. There's a lot of phony-baloney advice out there about how to find the optimal selling point in a particular stock, but when you're running a portfolio, there is just one criterion to keep in mind—namely, is there some stock *outside* your portfolio that you like better than something that's inside? If the answer is yes, the sell decision becomes automatic.

The hard part, believe it or not, is to look at your sell decisions in this broader context. But if you're only looking for indicators that emanate solely from the stock you're considering selling, you're leaving out an important piece of the portfolio management puzzle. We've seen that contrarians can sell too soon, and that tendency certainly has to be checked. But if you've found another turnaround story that you deem to have even greater potential than the last, what are you waiting for? Even if you can't find an earth-shattering fault with one of your existing holdings, it doesn't belong in your portfolio if you really and truly favor something else.

Remember, selling is almost never a psychologically rewarding event, which relates to a fundamental and poorly understood asymmetry of the market process. Whereas we usually don't mind not *buying* at the absolute low, because in a literal sense that's utterly unrealistic (you shouldn't have sworn off IBM at $45 in 1993 just because it was at ten cents in 1933), we get it into our heads that selling isn't good unless we get a terrific price—higher than any other price we could have gotten during our ownership. Unfortunately, by this reckoning, the only satisfying sales are those of a stock that completely tanks two days after our sale, an event otherwise known as pure luck.

If it's any comfort, consider that some of the great investment moves of this century created downright embarrassing individual decisions on the sell side. Around the time of World War II, John Templeton amassed every stock he could that was trading at $1 or less, figuring they would be disproportionate winners in peacetime. Sure enough, he was able to sell at an average price of between $3 and $4 just a few years later. A couple of the stocks he sold moved on to $100 or more, but those individual sell-too-soon mistakes came in the context of a sensational maneuver for the portfolio as a whole. Benjamin Graham could tell a similar story with regard to his criterion to sell after a 50 percent gain; the stock frequently disobeyed the stop sign and went far higher, but Graham didn't mind as long as his system uncovered other attractive stocks in which to invest the proceeds.

Psychological Diversification

Diversify your portfolio, by all means, but do it purposefully, not just because you heard it was the right thing to do. In particular, you don't have to own oil stocks, airline stocks, or forest products stocks just because there's a spot open for them. If you don't understand an industry well, you're better off staying away from it entirely, rather than investing in it just to round out your portfolio.

As a corollary, you might find that as you fill your portfolio one stock at a time, certain areas become disproportionately represented. Don't panic, at least not yet. It could be that your overweighting is entirely appropriate because the overweighted area of the market, whether it be technology or interest-sensitive stocks, might well represent unusual value. If that's the case, your portfolio will surely outperform those who artificially restrict their holdings of any one market sector.

But in keeping with this book's focus, I strongly recommend that you diversify your portfolio in terms of personality as well as by industry group, particularly if you find you've been getting in your own way. For example, a contrarian might feel diversified with a portfolio consisting of Kmart, Reebok, Advanced Micro Devices, Halliburton, and Data General, but look again. Each of these companies ranks number two or lower in its respective industry. The contrarian streak is found in every selection, and in that respect the portfolio isn't diversified at all. If you compared the performance of that portfolio with one consisting of Wal-Mart, Nike, Intel, Schlumberger, and IBM, you'd find out whether the contrarianism was a help or a hindrance. If it's the latter, some personality based diversification could be the perfect solution.

Experiments You Can Try at Home

There's another piece of advice that I might as well give here because you won't read it anywhere else: *The portfolio can be a terrific place for experimentation.* If you feel that you get in your own way, then try violating your own instincts once in a while—in a limited way, of course. Sometimes the only way to set our bad habits straight is to live on the other side for a while and realize that things aren't as bad as they seem. They might even be better.

That's why I have goaded sentimentalists to invest in companies that they can't stand but that objectively have a promising future. The idea is that those companies will become the sentimental choice of the *next* generation. Whatever category you represent, consider devoting 20 percent of your portfolio to experimentation of this sort. If that figure seems too high, then try experimenting with electronic portfolios instead. But make sure your portfolio doesn't represent "the same old thing," unless, of course, that same old thing is working like a charm. I am not asking anyone to change a winning game.

FINAL GAME PLAN

You're nearing the end of the book. Congratulations. I hope you've enjoyed it. I also hope I've imparted what I wanted to be the book's main message—we as investors should be constantly on the outlook for occasions when we get in our own way.

In that sense the advice in this book is as simple as the proverbial conversation between a patient and a doctor: "Doc, it only hurts when I do that." Replies the doctor, "Then don't do that."

If we as investors can identify precisely what it is that we do too much of, or too little of, we're on the way to recovery. The only missing step is to do something about it.

Avoiding Mismatches

If we fully understand ourselves, we won't blunder into stylistic mismatches, an investor's worst enemy. Some of the most routine situations described in this book have mismatch potential written all over them.

Conservative bargain hunters can wander into risky low P/E stocks. In-flexible investors use the excuse "I can always get back in later" when selling a perfectly good stock, only to wind up never taking themselves up on their own offer. Long-term investors can be attracted to companies with explosive earnings momentum, only to find that their accustomed strategy of holding on doesn't work well when the momentum runs its course.

"If only I knew what I was getting in to." Have you ever said that? May you never have to say it again.

I should make it clear that the benefits of using the portfolio as a place for experimentation can be lost if mismatches result. But it should also be clear that there is a big difference between knowingly adopting new strategies and accidentally creating piecemeal versions of them. The portfolio doesn't have to be uniform, but its pieces have to be consistent. When I was growing up, my family had dogs, cats, horses, and sheep. And we never confused one group with another.

Taking Corrective Action

If your investment choices aren't working, you should certainly consider making an adjustment. But remember that taking corrective action almost by definition means doing something that seems counterintuitive.

I remember seeing film clips of a 1950s TV routine by comedian Ernie Kovacs, who was an early master of that TV staple known as the sight gag. In one such gag, he set up a table on an incline and affixed a drinking glass to it. Then the camera was likewise tilted, so that when Kovacs brought a pitcher of milk seemingly directly over the glass and began pouring, he overshot his target, again and again.

Finally, he made an adjustment. He pulled the pitcher back away from the glass and began pouring. His effort may have appeared doomed to the TV audience, but it produced the desired result of having the milk go into the glass. All of which is to say that sometimes you have to adjust your thinking based on how it fits to the real world, even if part of you still clings to the notion that you were right the first time around.

In the stock market, corrective measures can be controversial. Consider the slogan "Invest, then investigate," which dates back to the go-go markets of the late 1960s, and which gets played out by adventurists to this very day. The idea behind the slogan was that with the market flying, you had more to lose by being out than by being in. Well, this approach fell flat on its face when the go-go era was gone, the moral being that you should never invest blindly, no matter how strong the market seems to be. You have to do some research before committing a dime. I doubt I'd find anyone to disagree.

However, suppose that even though you research all your ideas before purchasing, you find that you *always* end up buying. The probable reason for this rubber-stamping is a circumstance we looked at in the beginning of this book—that people's minds are often made up in advance, and as a result their research is cursory and inadequate. Adventurists and traders are particularly susceptible to this problem. For these investors, I might recommend "investing then investigating," and I could even do it with a straight face. The idea behind this corrective measure is that by making a small investment first, thereby getting the buying itch out of the way, the ensuing research might be rendered more legitimate. If the company still passes muster, you can always add to your initial purchase, right? This approach might generate some needless brokerage commissions for stocks that didn't satisfy that higher level of scrutiny, but if those were the same stocks you formerly lost your shirt on, you will come out ahead.

Not all adjustments have to be controversial. We've seen that for bargain hunters, making an adjustment might mean simply realizing that even though they were taught never to buy a stock at over 10 times earnings, that lesson came when interest rates were at 17 percent. Making an adjustment doesn't mean selling yourself out, and if you take that view you're a step behind already. If you need to change, then the first change should be in your semantic approach. Refer to adjustments by using words such as *experience, flexibility,* and *adaptation.* Sounds better already, doesn't it?

If you aren't getting in your own way, a different type of congratulations is in order. Keep up the good work. I've talked about a lot of pitfalls in this book, and you don't need to take corrective action unless they apply to you personally. So if you're a sentimentalist at heart but never make the mistake of hanging on to yesterday's stocks too long, then you needn't worry that other sentimentalists fall into that trap. That's their problem.

Above all, try to remember those occasions where you identified strongly with a psychological issue in this book. For that matter, remember those occasions where you outright disagreed or found the observations at odds with your personal experience. The issue isn't necessarily who's right and who's wrong. The goal is for every reader of this book to learn more about what drives his or her investment choices.

And if there were too many examples in this book to handle all at once, by all means reread the sections of greatest personal interest. Better yet, buy another book and start from the beginning—there might be salsa stains somewhere on this copy. If you put the book away for a few years, that's okay, too. But remember that over time, the specific stocks I've mentioned will become part of stock market history. They may lose their timeliness, but the underlying messages are intended to endure. If you understand your stock market personality, you're way ahead of the game. Here's wishing you the greatest possible success in carving out your own stock market destiny.

INDEX